THE TRUTH IS

1. Leveling up your craft to write a story that lives long after you've left the planet is what some might call a ridiculous goal.

2. You know that you will not tell that story after reading just one how-to-write book.

3. You know that you will not tell that story as the result of taking one seminar.

4. You know that creating a timeless work of art will require the dedication of a world-class athlete. You will be training your mind with as much ferocity and single-minded purpose as an Olympic gold medal hopeful. That kind of cognitive regimen excites you, but you just haven't found a convincing storytelling dojo to do that work.

5. The path to leveling up your creative craft is a dark and treacherous course. You've been at it a long time, and it often feels like you're wearing three-dimensional horse blinders. More times than you'd wish to admit, you're not sure if you are moving north or south or east or west. And the worst part? You can't see anyone else, anywhere going through what you're going through. You're all alone.

WELCOME TO THE STORY GRID UNIVERSE. HERE'S HOW WE CONTEND WITH THOSE TRUTHS:

1. We believe we find meaning in the pursuit of creations that last longer than we do. It is not ridiculous. Dedicating our work to seizing opportunities and overcoming obstacles as we stretch ourselves to reach for seemingly unreachable creations is transformational. We believe this pursuit is the most valuable and honorable way to spend our time here. Even if...especially if...we never reach our lofty creative goals.

2. Writing just one story isn't going to take us to the top. We're moving from point A to Point A^{5000}. We've got lots of mountains to climb, lots of rivers and oceans to cross, and many deep dark forests to traverse in our way. We need topographic guides on demand, and if they're not available now, we'll have to figure it out and write them ourselves.

3. While we're drawn to seminars to consume the imparted wisdom from an icon in the arena, we leave with something far more valuable than the curriculum. We get to meet the universe's other pilgrims and compare notes on the terrain.

4. The Story Grid Universe has a virtual dojo, a university to work out and get stronger—the place to stumble, correct the mistakes, and

stumble again until the moves become automatic, lethal, and mesmerizing to outside observers.

5. The Story Grid Universe has a performance space, a publishing house dedicated to leveling up the craft with clear boundaries of progress, and the ancillary reference resources to pack for each project mission. There is an infinite number of paths to where you want to be with a story that works.

Seeing how others made it down their own private yellow brick roads to release their creations into the timeless creative cosmos will help keep you on the straight and narrow path.

All are welcome—the more, the merrier—but please abide by the golden rule.

Put the Work Above All Else, and trust the process.

THE TIPPING POINT BY MALCOLM GLADWELL

A STORY GRID MASTERWORK ANALYSIS GUIDE

LESLIE WATTS
SHELLEY SPERRY

STORY GRID

STORY GRID

Story Grid Publishing LLC
223 Egremont Plain Road
PMB 191
Egremont, MA 01230

First Story Grid Publishing Paperback Edition March 2020

For Information About Special Discounts for Bulk Purchases,

Please visit www.storygridpublishing.com

ISBN: 978-1-64501-045-6
Ebook: 978-1-64501-046-3

For

All Past, Present, and Future Story Nerds

INTRODUCTION

Thinking as Adventure

Many Big Idea books originate with a writer's sudden "aha moment."

You're thinking about a particular phenomenon or problem you're interested in, and you look at it from a new angle that leads to some insights you've never had before. You get excited and can't stop thinking about it. It's not a fully formed idea—not by a long shot; there are so many complications and questions to work out. But you've stepped over a threshold of sorts, and you're on a new intellectual journey.

This exploratory impulsive motion is why readers (and writers) love Big Idea books. They turn thinking into an adventure.

The first steps on the Big Idea writer's adventure look something like this. You notice the phenomenon or problem and decide to investigate. You ask friends and experts about it, consult research studies, and take note of compelling anecdotes about those experiences. At some point, you drag yourself away from the research and record the raw results of your investigation—3x5 cards, notebooks, scraps of paper, digital files—and you start to gather your thoughts. As you're working to detect recurring patterns, you get frustrated. Frequently, the evidence and anecdotes lead you to detours that appear to be dead ends. After a while, you can't remember why you said "aha!" in the first place.

But then a piece of evidence falls into place and provides a nexus to a working hypothesis that explains the phenomenon or solves the problem. The seemingly unrelated data points coalesce. The "aha" turns into Eureka!

You're not done, not even close, but you find yourself invigorated. You get your second wind. You now test your hypothesis many times to see if it works in different circumstances. You tweak it a little as you bring in new evidence and case studies.

Finally, after you've triumphed over a few more doubts and challenges, you think you've come to the end of the adventure, and you've got an idea that explains the phenomenon or solves the problem you've been battling.

But now you have a whole new challenge. You need to bring your knowledge home and share it with other people. You must describe the process by which you came to your conclusion compellingly. Then you have to prescribe a means by which the reader can use this new insight as a powerful tool in their everyday life.

How are you going to present all your work to those who can benefit from your intellectual dragon-slaying? You're going to have to embark on one more adventure. You're going to have to write a book.

And you're going to need the help of a good mentor—a model of excellence—on the next part of this journey.

If you read a lot of Big Idea books, as we do, you know many brilliant mentors are writing today: Malcolm Gladwell, Brené Brown, Elizabeth Gilbert, and Michael Pollan, just to name a few. The way they become true mentors has nothing to do with trying to wrangle a coffee date with them or harassing them on Twitter. What's remarkable about the Story Grid methodology is that you can apply it to these mentors' works.

The works themselves can serve as the models for you to emulate, not the quirky human beings who crafted them. Let's leave these writers in peace to keep pursuing the adventures that fascinate them. Instead, we'll study the products of those intellectual adventures.

We won't just read their books. We'll put them under a microscope and observe them with a telescope. We'll break them down into their constituent parts and build them back up again to their global gestalts. We'll analyze them to see how they work.

In other words, we'll follow the same process you would use to explore and refine your own Big Idea. This step-by-step method is how The Story Grid Masterwork series approaches mentorship. We study the work and hold it up as our model, a map providing detailed topography and directions we can use to guide us when we set out on our own artist journeys.

When contemplating our first Big Idea masterwork, we naturally zeroed in on Malcolm Gladwell's seminal book, *The Tipping Point*. We believe Gladwell's book epitomizes the best practices of the form. What are those?

Using the Story Grid methodology developed by Shawn Coyne, and building on his blog post series at www.storygrid.com about *The Tipping Point*, we decided to plumb the depths of Gladwell's masterwork from our unique points of view to find out.

As Story Grid Certified Editors who love working with Big Idea book authors, we're in the trenches day in and day out figuring out how best to help writers at an impasse. We're applying the method practically, and we have a hands-on "let's get this thing to work" approach to the analysis.

So, we want to share with you some of what we've learned from Shawn Coyne, Malcolm Gladwell, and our favorite authors and clients, in the hope that you'll be able to put it to use in bringing your own book into the world.

The Power of Big Ideas

When you read a book like *The Tipping Point*, the way you think about a problem or a phenomenon in the world changes, your mind expands a little, and sometimes the ground beneath your feet seems to shift. Big Idea books are fundamentally about exploration, revelation, and the creation of knowledge that didn't exist before. So, naturally, this is why the life value at stake in any Big Idea book is all about the journey from ignorance to wisdom—or even self-deception to wisdom.

Big idea books change us, and by extension, they change the world. In *The Fire Next Time*, James Baldwin started a new conversation about racism and relationships that continues more than half a century later. The same is true of Rachel Carson, who reframed our thinking about nature in *Silent Spring* and helped birth the modern environmental movement. And in *Chaos*, James Gleick introduced the world to a whole new science, explaining how minuscule changes produce massive transformations in complex systems. More recently, in *Being Mortal*, Atul Gawande revolutionized the way we think about and experience death and dying.

The Tipping Point, one of the most read Big Idea books in recent years, explores how social epidemics spread, or tip, just like disease epidemics do. Author Malcolm Gladwell was fascinated by a particular phenomenon that all of us had accepted as "just the way it is." He set himself a mission to explore what was beneath that phenomenon, and he decided to take us on that journey with him. He wanted to understand why ideas, products, messages, and behaviors suddenly seem ubiquitous, when only months, days, or even hours before, they were rare.

Gladwell wanted to know what causal events preceded a thing "tipping" into the forefront of a culture's collective awareness.

A really cool exploratory mission to be sure, but how would he tell this complex story?

The answers lie within the work itself.

The Macro and Micro Structures of a Big Idea Nonfiction Book

If you're a writer who loves toying with ideas, gathering lots of research and anecdotes, and provoking readers to experience a revelation through story—while also teaching them how to make or do something along the way—studying *The Tipping Point's* structure, both globally and scene by scene, is the masterclass you need.

Let's start with the telescopic point of view.

If we look at Big Idea books in general terms, we can see three clear steps in the intellectual adventure stories they tell: analyzing, formalizing, and mechanizing.

These parts correspond to the beginning, middle, and end of every compelling Big Idea story:

1. **Beginning Hook:** This section is all about analyzing the phenomenon and finding intriguing patterns shared among its multiple iterations. In other words, you hook the reader by offering them a series of examples of a recurring event and asking, "Do you ever wonder why this happens?" The Beginning Hook culminates in a hypothesis. "This happens because of X, Y, or Z." Imagine you see some intriguing new electric cars, which you've never noticed before, rolling down the street. You eventually figure out how they work and decide to present your findings to your friends. You entice your friends with a taste of what you've discovered. This analysis hook usually accounts for the first 10 percent or so of the book.

2. **Middle Build:** Formalizing the analysis into a system that explains how the phenomenon or problem is structured, how it functions, and how it is organized happens in the Middle Build. Formalizing brings evidence and reason to bear to reveal a phenomenon's structural and functional organization. The Middle Build is the longest part of any Big Idea book—as much as 80 percent. In this section you take the phenomenon or problem apart and lay all of its constitutive pieces out on your intellectual lawn like one of those cars. Then, as you consult with some experts and research, you slowly put the phenomenon back together to see if you can start it up again.

3. **Ending Payoff:** Mechanizing the explanation so others can use it as a tool is how your work culminates in the Ending Payoff. You do this by generating the feature list of parts of the phenomenon and presenting strategies and tactics to jump-start its recurrence or build more just like it. Finally, in this last 10 percent of the book, you're able to help readers see how they can understand the phenomenon or problem like you do and use that knowledge to their benefit.

Armed with this understanding of the basic structure, let's now study how Malcolm Gladwell's *The Tipping Point* abides by these global macro concepts.

Malcolm Gladwell's Big Ideas

The New Yorker journalist Malcolm Gladwell defined a particular kind of nonfiction book in the early twenty-first century when he came out with one bestselling sociological deep dive after another: *The Tipping Point* (2000), *Blink* (2005), and *Outliers* (2008).

While some Big Idea authors write about social problems they want to solve, Gladwell writes about phenomena he wants to understand and explain. In an approach that's now labeled "Gladwellian," he sniffs out funny and heartbreaking anecdotes, synthesizes reams of academic research, identifies fascinating experts, and then builds an argument that explains the phenomenon that's obsessed him while also offering advice about how to apply his lessons learned.

Ever since the emergence of his commercial and literary success, Gladwell has been criticized for relying too much on anecdotes and not enough on data. His work is now often described as unscientific and imperfect by ivory tower experts. We believe this criticism, while valuable to refresh and refine his work, does not detract from Gladwell's original artistry. At no point does Gladwell claim he's putting forth a "be all" and "end all" hypothesis. He would be the last one to call himself an expert.

Gladwell represents himself authentically as one who values anecdotes and stories as essential in the pursuit of wisdom. Although not an academic himself, he seeks out PhDs and other authorities to guide him along his way. This very quality of being an amateur who enlists the help of experts sets popular Big Idea authors apart from academic authors.

The author of a Big Idea book is trying to simplify a lot of theories and conclusions that scientists, social scientists, and other researchers developed over many years through rigorous analysis and experimentation. Big Idea authors strive to make sense of that academic arcana and translate those complex ideas for a broad, popular audience. These works represent one person's quest to make sense of our very complicated world.

In a 2019 interview, Gladwell reveals why he does what he does and the fact that his work—and the work of all Big Idea writers—is always imperfect:

> I like discovering things. What happens is, I keep going back and discovering that what I thought five years ago isn't right. It's incomplete. The idea that part of what it means to be human in the world and a thinking person is to constantly be correcting your beliefs is, to me, fascinating and addictive...It makes thinking an adventure.[1]

We think the most valuable lesson any writer can draw from Gladwell is how important it is to acknowledge and even celebrate your own imperfection. You'll make mistakes, change your mind, find new evidence, and question your ideas again and again. That's not only okay, it's essential.

Sometimes you will interpret information in new ways that don't jibe with the original research or with follow-up studies. As Gladwell admits in the quote above, his thinking is never set in stone; it evolves as he discovers more, as we see in the Afterword of *The Tipping Point* (in our analysis, scene 52). This need for constant rethinking and revision is one of the hazards and pleasures you'll discover in writing a Big Idea book.

There's one more lesson to take from Gladwell early in your process. Take your ideas out for a trial run. Lots of Big Idea books begin as articles in magazines or newspapers that balloon into tens of thousands of words because the author falls in love with the ideas and just can't quit them, which was the case with *The Tipping Point*. It grew from a few *New Yorker* articles Gladwell wrote in the 1990s.

Testing and honing your idea in short articles or presentations in front of audiences is the perfect way to find out whether readers are as interested in it as you are—or to put it in Gladwell's terms, whether your ideas are "sticky."

A Three-in-One Genre

Another defining global characteristic and challenge of Big Idea nonfiction is that it integrates three nonfiction categories into one. It's similar to the Thriller genre in fiction, which incorporates the Action, Horror, and Crime genres. Another way to think of it is that a Big Idea book is a little like an Avengers story in the Marvel Universe—one in which the heroes temporarily leave their separate worlds and assemble to work as a team. So let's meet these three nonfiction players.

The three types of nonfiction that you assemble into a Big Idea book are:

1. **Narrative nonfiction.** Fiction's story structure is the star of narrative nonfiction, which uses tricks of the novelist's trade, including richly detailed characters and dramatic conflicts, to bring events alive. Although most narrative nonfiction works (histories, biographies, investigative journalism, memoirs) have controlling or big ideas to convey, they are built around the progression of a story, not an explanation of those ideas. The narrative journey matters most.

2. **Academic nonfiction.** Small groups of specialists hold each other to a high standard of evidence and analysis in scholarly books and articles, usually through the peer review process. Almost by definition, academic works lack a strong author voice because the information and analysis are most important, not the individual voice or emotional connection with an audience. Analysis and formalizing compelling hypotheses matter most.

3. **How-to nonfiction.** Like academic nonfiction, these books target a specific audience with valuable information. But in this case, the books are translations of a sort. Authors help ordinary people without degrees or special skills understand how to make, become, or survive something in a step-by-step prescriptive process. Mechanization is all.

When we read *The Tipping Point*, we can see how Gladwell makes use of the distinctive elements in each of these three genres. He tells us stories that make us care about people from the streets of Baltimore to California's skateparks. He digs into data. He analyzes that data to support an argument like an academic, and he shows us how people have applied the lessons of *The Tipping Point* so we can do that too.

Life Values

Any Big Idea book, including *The Tipping Point*, is an account of a revelation. It tracks the author's step-by-step journey from ignorance to wisdom, as they investigate a particular question or problem. This progression forms the core of the story and injects narrative drive—the quality that makes a reader keep turning pages.

This progressive change along a continuum from ignorance to wisdom is what we call a *life value shift*, and is one of the most important concepts to keep in mind as you write each scene of your book. In our analysis of *The Tipping Point* below, we'll make careful note of the most critical life values that change in every scene. This is important because if your scenes do not embody change, readers will lose interest.

A life value is a human condition or experience that can change from positive to negative, negative to positive, negative to more negative, and positive to more positive. When you write or analyze a scene, you have to first ask yourself: What life value changes here? Most often in Big Idea books, that change happens on the ignorance-wisdom spectrum. (See the Foolscap for various points along this spectrum.) But sometimes a scene or a beat within a scene in a Big Idea book will focus on a particular illustrative story, and in that case, the life value will change along another continuum, such as death-life. That would be the case in the teen suicide stories Gladwell cites (in our analysis, scene 44).

Other Global Components of Big Idea Nonfiction

Let's now take a look at the "must-have" elements of Big Idea books, or what Shawn Coyne defines as Conventions and Obligatory Scenes. How does Gladwell make use of them to satisfy his readers' expectations while still surprising and engaging us at every turn?

Conventions and Obligatory Scenes in Big Idea Nonfiction

If you're acquainted with Story Grid's approach to fiction, you will know about the Conventions and Obligatory Scenes of fiction genres. In a work of fiction, conventions are the characters, settings, and means of turning the plot that set up reader expectations for the genre and establish the global life value. They create the conditions for a particular kind of change in a story—and we know stories are all about change.

Obligatory Scenes are events, revelations, and decisions that pay off reader expectations and turn the global life value. If Conventions set up the conditions for change, the Obligatory Scenes are the cause of a particular change in a story.

In nonfiction, Conventions and Obligatory Scenes operate in almost the same way as in fiction.

In Big Idea Nonfiction:

- Conventions are the ingredients needed to create the global life value shift, which is always on the spectrum of ignorance to knowledge to wisdom.
- Obligatory Scenes explore questions that turn the global life value from ignorance to knowledge to wisdom.

CONVENTIONS

A Cast of Characters

To effectively tell the story of how your knowledge came to be, you will need a cast of characters. These are:

Author-protagonist: The author is the protagonist or hero in Big Idea books, and by extending a hand to us and taking us on a step-by-step journey of discovery, we readers are, by extension, the protagonists and heroes too. Unlike academic authors, Big Idea authors often reveal quite a lot about themselves in their writing, fleshing out the protagonist to gain readers' empathy. In *The Tipping Point*, the character of Gladwell is an author-journalist, a curious nerd, a New Yorker transplanted from Canada, and a man with lots of exciting and important friends who find their way into several chapters.

Sidekicks: These are the characters who exemplify particular components of the global hypothesis or idea. In *The Tipping Point*, Gladwell introduces the reader to many everyday people, including Roger Horchow, Lois Weisberg, and Mark Alpert, each of whom represents one of the building blocks of his ideas.

Villain or Force of Antagonism: The villain or force of antagonism in a Big Idea book is the roadblock, or what stands in the way of understanding the phenomenon or solving the problem. Shawn explains that "*The Tipping Point* has the most dastardly villain of them all ... an unbeatable one to boot ... The villain of *The Tipping Point* (and all of Big Idea nonfiction for that matter) is the human condition."[2] The author must vanquish human ignorance and weakness to finish the journey toward wisdom.

Setting: The setting is the global arena in which the problem or phenomenon operates, generally a significant internal or external canvas. In *The Tipping Point*, Gladwell is looking at why ideas, products, messages, and behaviors go viral. His setting spans many decades and much of the world—from 1775 in New England, where a revolutionary message with the right messenger went viral, to Sesame Street in the 1960s, where education got "sticky," to New York City in the 1990s, where violent crime trends "tipped" for the better.

Means of Turning the Point

The structural, functional organization of the Big Idea hypothesis often defies conventional wisdom. We think a phenomenon is caused by X, but it's really caused by Y. That is, the Big Idea author-protagonist's hypothesis or theory is most intriguing when it is counterintuitive. In *The Tipping Point*, Gladwell tells us within the first few pages that "Ideas and products and messages and behaviors spread just like viruses do."[3] Nearly two decades after Gladwell published his book, this seems so obvious, but when he first shared it, this was a radically different way of thinking about rapid change. His book upturned conventional wisdom, added a new term to our everyday vocabulary, and stayed on the bestseller lists for years.

Forms of Argument: Ethos, Logos, and Pathos. Every Big Idea book uses three classic forms of argument to persuade readers. The arena or subject of the book usually determines the type of persuasion that is used most frequently and effectively.

Ethos relies on the bona fides of the author and whether they are someone readers should trust. Do they have experience or some form of expertise in the arena in which they are writing? Gladwell's credentials come from a long career as a journalist and his position on the staff of one of America's most respected magazines.

Logos depends on evidence, data, and all the experts and observers the author gathers to support his conclusions about the structural, functional organization (the essence of) the phenomenon. As you'll see in the Story Grid Spreadsheet for *The Tipping Point*, the experts on which Gladwell relies range from car salesmen to social scientists. His data and story-based evidence are equally varied. After dismantling the phenomenon into its constituent parts, he puts it all back together again thoughtfully, coherently, and artfully.

Pathos relies on an appeal to the emotions of the audience, arousing anger or tears or appealing to their self-interest or sense of identity. In this form of argument, the storytelling techniques of fiction are crucial to success. When he begins a chapter packed with statistics and scientific studies about the contagious behaviors of teen suicide and smoking, Gladwell lays aside ethos and logos for a few pages and tells one of the most compelling stories in his book—the story of a boy named Sima. It's a short, simple story, but it has a clear beginning, middle, and end. The end is a heartbreaking suicide note.[4] That story engages readers emotionally and carries us through the rest of the chapter, searching for answers. Gladwell, who is not a father himself, talks at several points in the same chapter about "our children" and "our teens," providing a reminder amid all the objective evidence, that there are human lives at stake, including the lives of children and teens we all know.

Multiple points of view. And what about the narrative device, or in other words, who is telling the story? Gladwell uses the same narrative device in almost every book, article, speech, and podcast episode, and it has become his trademark. In Shawn Coyne's words, Gladwell's narrative device is "a nerd who likes to figure things out."[5] Rather than a pedantic or detached narrator, he is a smart and curious friend, and that's one of the secrets of his success.

The arena or subject matter of the book will also determine the point of view or multiple points of view. As you'll notice on the spreadsheet that accompanies this analysis, most scenes in *The Tipping Point* include several points of view. These include third-person omniscient (the most authoritative point of view), first-person omniscient, and first-person plural.[6] Gladwell is notorious for bringing in stories and characters from his own life and giving up the objective voice of a journalist when it's helpful. He even uses second-person singular. (If you're trying to engage readers in a conversation with your ideas fully, second person is an especially valuable tool. We're using it a lot in the book you're reading now.)

Narrative cliffhangers. In addition to employing pathos in their arguments, Big Idea authors must make use of other tools of the novelist that create narrative drive (mystery, suspense, and dramatic irony).[7] Without narrative drive, a Big Idea book won't hold the readers' interest, and they'll never reach the Big Reveal. Big Idea writers keep us glued to the page by regulating the amount of information they provide —not too much and not too little.

In *The Tipping Point*, we think we know the payoff of the book from the Beginning Hook. Gladwell states his Big Idea upfront, but the evidence and stories that clarify and amplify Gladwell's idea come in small, progressively complicating steps, each of which carries its own little bit of mystery. Every American schoolchild knows the story of Paul Revere. However, in Gladwell's telling, he's still able to create suspense around exactly how the message that "The British are coming!" reached hundreds of sleepy townsfolk. And the Ending Payoff of *The Tipping Point* is inevitable and surprising too.

Set Pieces or Sequences. Mini stories within the global Big Idea story include a dilemma that must be solved before the global quest for wisdom can move forward. Often, writers need to build sequences of stories to lead readers toward their more complex conclusions. For example, Gladwell must convince us to understand and accept the "Power of Context" if we're going to understand and accept the Big Idea, and he does so in a six-scene sequence.

In chapter 4, Gladwell starts building his case for the "Power of Context," which is so critical to the rest of his argument. He recounts specific details of Bernhard Goetz's shooting of four black youths on the New York subway, which represented a low point in the city's history of crime (in our analysis, scene 29). Gladwell follows this close-up of a single crime by zooming out to provide a panoramic view of New York City (in our analysis, scene 30). Next, Gladwell explains crime as an epidemic capable of tipping and how the "Power of Context" contributes to that causal happening (in our analysis, scene 31). Readers see how this concept was applied in New York City to cause crime to tip for the better, and how it explains what happened in the case of Goetz and the four youths (in our analysis, scene 32). Finally, Gladwell explains why the connection between context and crime is so hard for us to believe by recounting a few additional examples (in our analysis, scenes 33 and 34).

Just these few scenes demonstrate Gladwell's mastery, but if we look at the book as a whole, his storytelling craft is even more impressive. The external stakes in each sequence escalate, just as they would in a thriller or adventure novel. Gladwell doesn't begin with the set-piece about suicides in Micronesia. He builds from entertaining tales about Hush Puppies and successful crime-fighting in New York to more disturbing stories that are essential to understanding epidemics. He knows that leading with more complex and grim examples would create a barrier to the reader's acceptance of his ideas. The lesson here is that not only do the evidence and stories you choose make your book compelling but so does the order in which you choose to deliver that evidence.

External Genre Conventions. The main story in a Big Idea book is an internal one, but there is also an external story. Most books have both an internal genre, which tracks the protagonist's inner psychological journey, and an external genre, which tracks external forces (other people, society, the environment) that create conflicts for the protagonist.[8]

The external genre in a Big Idea book can be challenging to identify because the internal quest for knowledge is so powerful. In *The Tipping Point*, the stakes are often life or death, as Gladwell describes the spread of disease epidemics and social epidemics like smoking and suicide.

One way to look at the external genre of *The Tipping Point* is to see it as an Action story in which the author and reader are not only the heroes, but also the victims. Gladwell writes about his missteps and the way data and his informants thwart his efforts to understand the way products and ideas "tip." He's a sort of intellectual Action superhero in a fight against ignorance as he gathers the bits of knowledge like Infinity stones that will eventually transform into wisdom.

Obligatory Scenes

Establish the problem or phenomenon. The author-protagonist introduces the reader to the problem or phenomenon they will explore. In *The Tipping Point*, Gladwell introduces us to the phenomenon of dramatic, rapid, and unexplained change through two very different examples from the 1990s: Hush Puppies shoes, a brand that was dying before it suddenly went viral, and New York City's crime statistics, which tipped for the better.

A clear statement of the Big Idea early on. Authors must present their Big Idea and the arguments that support it in the Beginning Hook. Gladwell tells us in the third scene of *The Tipping Point* that "Ideas and products and messages and behaviors spread just like viruses do." He lays the groundwork for his three rules of Tipping Points (the Law of the Few, Stickiness, and the Power of Context) early in the book too, introducing the mechanisms by which the phenomenon emerges alongside the thesis statement and heightening the mystery or narrative drive. The reader can't help but think, "What are those three things all about?" The reader's curiosity gets them to turn the next page.

Evidence that supports the Big Idea. Academic research, experiments, studies, and analysis are crucial foundational evidence in a Big Idea book, as are interviews with experts in the field. Throughout the Middle Build, Gladwell presents the research of social scientists, historians, and other scholars that slowly builds his argument about how Tipping Points work, carrying readers forward to the Big Reveal in the Ending Payoff. Analysis of Paul Revere (chapter 2), *Blue's Clues* (chapter 3), and the magic number 150 (chapter 5) figure prominently. Gladwell then shares even more specific case studies to solidify readers' understanding of his Big Idea (chapters 6 and 7).

Entertaining or compelling anecdotes. Scenes that are funny, shocking, touching, or otherwise entertaining have become obligatory in modern Big Idea books. Think of them as fodder for great conversations with friends, coworkers, and family. Gladwell made his name as a master of the juicy anecdote—a talent he recently turned into a new career as a podcast host. In *The Tipping Point*, for example, he tells us in great detail how the creators of *Blue's Clues* built on the success of *Sesame Street* to make learning even stickier. He brings the characters in each anecdote to life in just a few paragraphs—from Mark Alpert and his genius for choosing hotels and cars to a Chinese teacher mistaken for a spy. Remember that every memorable story you share helps readers later recall and discuss your Big Idea.

How-to advice. Every Big Idea book includes prescriptive information so readers will know how to apply the knowledge they've gained. Gladwell's conclusion (our analysis, scene 51) shows us how Georgia Sadler used the rules of Tipping Points (the Law of the Few, Stickiness, and the Power of Context) and applied key lessons (focused efforts, testing intuition, and hope) to pursue a successful campaign to spread awareness of breast cancer and diabetes within the black community in San Diego. By using this positive how-to example, Gladwell convinces us we can tip change in a positive direction. The message is a hopeful one: "Tipping Points are a reaffirmation of the potential for change and the power of intelligent action."[9]

Big Reveal. This obligatory scene is the Core Event of the Big Idea book, in which the author-protagonist reveals a twist or more profound understanding of the phenomenon or problem, often convincing us that what we've believed in the past is all wrong. In *The Tipping Point*, that revelation is a warning about the destructive power of Tipping Points. Gladwell suggests that although "tipping" a product, behavior, or idea from obscurity to ubiquity can be a positive phenomenon (the rise of Hush Puppies and decline of New York Crime), it also has a dark side.[10] The charismatic Connectors, Mavens, and Salespeople Gladwell describes throughout the book can also push nihilistic messages that lead to self-destructive and violent behavior (teen smoking, suicide, and mass shootings).

Still, even in the twist of his Big Reveal, Gladwell can't help but end on a note that elevates his faith in knowledge and wisdom, the very life values he's been pursuing throughout the book. He urges his readers to put their own new knowledge and understanding to work. Although we live in a world that is "volatile and inexplicable," he admits in the final paragraph, "Tipping Points are a reaffirmation of the potential for change and the power of intelligent action. Look at the world around you. It may seem like an immovable, implacable place. It is not. With the slightest push—in just the right place—it can be tipped."[11]

User Advice for Our Guide to *The Tipping Point*

This Guide includes four parts beyond this Introduction:

   1. A Story Grid Foolscap Page

   2. A Scene-by-Scene Spreadsheet

   3. A Story Grid Infographic

   4. Scene Analysis

   Items 1–3 can be found and downloaded here https://storygrid.com/masterwork/tipping-point, and the Scene Analysis follows below.

What's a Foolscap Page? The one-page Story Grid Foolscap is a bird's-eye view of the structure of *The Tipping Point*.

What's a Scene-by-Scene Spreadsheet? The scene-by-scene spreadsheet includes more granular structural details, including point of view, "sidekick characters," life value shifts, and locations.

What's a Story Grid Infographic? The Story Grid Infographic is a visual representation of the value shifts in the internal and external stories that combine to make up the global story.

What is Scene Analysis? In the Scene Analysis, you'll see each of the fifty-two scenes in the book analyzed in terms of their Inquiry Events and the Five Commandments of Storytelling.

A Few Words About Analyzing Scenes in a Big Idea Book

To define a scene in a work of fiction, you usually begin by asking yourself what the characters are doing, what they want, and how they change. In fiction, each scene is about conflict and change, even if the change is minor or only happens in the mind of one of the characters.

When you look at how individual scenes work in Big Idea books (or when writing your own), you'll often be tempted to focus on the details of the compelling anecdotal stories (Hush Puppies! Syphilis! Smoking!) because they feature the kinds of conflict and change we intuitively understand.

To bring yourself back to the big picture of the Big Idea book's progression, it's helpful to ask yourself two things:

1. What is the author-protagonist trying to do, show, or communicate about the Big Idea mentioned in the Beginning Hook/Introduction?
2. Why is the author-protagonist discussing this particular evidence (a story or some data) here and now?

By answering these questions, you'll be able to get to the heart of what's really happening in the nonfiction "scene."

A working scene in a Big Idea nonfiction book contains at least one Inquiry Event, which is an active change of life value along the

Ignorance—Knowledge—Wisdom spectrum. It represents the author-protagonist's stage in a progression to understand and mechanize the book's Big Idea. It can sometimes be hard to pinpoint because, as mentioned above, it's easy to be distracted by other exemplary stories happening in the scene.

The way to identify an Inquiry Event is to answer four questions:

1. What is the author-protagonist literally doing in the scene?

That's the Literal Action. For example, in the first scene of *The Tipping Point*, it's tempting to retell the details of cool kids wearing Hush Puppies in Manhattan and all that ensued as a result. But in fact, what's important can be summarized in just a sentence explaining that Gladwell is introducing a story about the rising popularity of the Hush Puppies brand from 1994 to 1995.

2. What is the author trying to accomplish in the scene?

That's the Essential Action. Again, in the case of this first scene, Gladwell is introducing his first big question for readers: "Why do certain products or ideas become popular overnight?"

3. What has changed along the Ignorance—Knowledge—Wisdom spectrum in the scene?

In the case of the first scene, Gladwell has gone from having no real compulsion to learning about Hush Puppies' sudden popularity to getting bitten by the curiosity bug. This narrative bug bite induces him to raise lots of questions and to recognize his own ignorance. So he, as the protagonist-narrator of the story, moves from Status Quo Worldview to Ignorance.

4. What is the resulting Inquiry Event?

And now it's possible to put together the Inquiry Event, or question, that expresses the whole point of this scene. How does a thirty-dollar pair of shoes go from a handful of Manhattan hipsters and designers to every mall in America in just two years? That question is the catnip to get readers to keep reading.

The Five Commandments

The Five Commandments of Storytelling in a Big Idea book are different from those in a narrative, story-driven book, so the way you apply them to scenes is a little different too.

This shifting five-command mindset is one of the most challenging things to wrap our heads around when we try to break down any Big Idea book, including *The Tipping Point*.

The Tipping Point is full of stories that illustrate how Gladwell made intellectual connections between shoes and epidemics or crime and bestselling novels. These stories are accessible to most readers and more fun to read than the dozens of academic papers Gladwell devoured in his quest to understand the concept of Tipping Points. So, it's tempting to focus on these stories when you're analyzing an inquiry event in a Big Idea scene.

You'll instinctively want to look for the 1) Inciting Incident, 2) Complications that culminate in a Turning Point/Phere, 3) Crisis, 4) Climax, and 5) Resolution just as you would in a traditional novel or piece of narrative nonfiction. (For a review of the Five Commandments of Storytelling, read one of Shawn Coyne's early blog posts.[12] And for an explanation at his evolving notion of the Turning Point Progressive Complication, or "Phere," listen to or read the transcript of *The Story Grid Podcast* episode "5 Commandments and Pheres."[13])

But in Big Idea nonfiction, the building blocks of your argument are questions and answers. In a novel or short story, scenes turn on conflicts that build toward a change for the protagonist. In a Big Idea book, scenes turn on questions and answers that build toward wisdom for the protagonist.

So let's look at how we define the Five Commandments of Storytelling in Big Idea nonfiction, which you'll see in all the scenes analyzed in the next section of this book:

Inciting Incident: The author-protagonist presents a story, event, or fact about a particular phenomenon that gives rise to a question.

Progressive Complications: The author-protagonist presents the results of their investigation of the question in the form of research or shoe-leather evidence (interviews with compelling experts in the domain).

Turning Point Progressive Complication/Phere: The author-protagonist finds new, unexpected evidence that sparks a revelation, which gives rise to a crisis.

Crisis: The author-protagonist faces a dilemma about how to integrate this unexpected evidence into the evolving hypothesis.

Climax: The author-protagonist resolves the Crisis by incorporating the unexpected evidence into their global hypothesis.

Resolution: The Resolution is a convincing recap of the evidence collected to answer the question raised by the inciting incident and how the author-protagonist made sense of it.

Our Surprising but Inevitable Conclusion

What's our takeaway and how-to advice for you as you start on your own Big Idea project? If you've had your aha or Eureka moment, but don't know where or how to start writing a book, you should keep reading works that inform and inspire you. Study the work of Gladwell here and analyze his other books, too, which are equally well-crafted.

Generally and generously apply the Story Grid methodology to the work of nonfiction masters you admire. We recommend books like Matthew Desmond's *Evicted*, Elizabeth Kolbert's *The Sixth Extinction*, Ta-Nehisi Coates's *Between the World and Me*, and Michael Pollan's *In Defense of Food*.

Gather your 3x5 cards and your laptop and use Story Grid tools to write and revise your work. Remember that your favorite writers started just like you: With a few ideas and some research—struggling, failing, changing, and struggling some more.

Something we mentioned above bears repeating: Some scholars and critics find fault with Gladwell's methods and the evidence he uses to support his Big Idea that "Ideas and products and messages and behaviors spread just like viruses do." And we know Gladwell himself says his ideas and conclusions have changed over the years. So let's focus on what a Big Idea book is by remembering what it isn't.

Academic books are the work of experts steeped in a subject for years or decades. They take primary sources, the raw material of experimentation and years of research, they vet the analysis and conclusions through peer review, and then they tell readers what they should think, based on all that acquired expertise.

But a Big Idea book encourages readers to think for themselves. Big Idea books are for people like us—curious non-experts who want to understand the world better. We are encouraged to look at a phenomenon or problem from a new angle, in other words, to see and think about it differently. This kind of book is the record of the author-protagonist's attempt to make sense of a phenomenon or find a solution to a problem in story form. It's a contribution to the trove of human knowledge. It's the gift an author brings back and shares at the end of their intellectual adventure.

Do we believe everything presented within *The Tipping Point* is the capital "T" truth? No, and textbooks don't fare so well on that score either. But does Gladwell help us see and think about the world in new and enlightening ways? Absolutely.

So, if you have a Big Idea you've been considering sharing with the world, accept the challenge of the intellectual adventure. You have a map, now get on your way.

~

For all the resources listed throughout this book, please visit:
https://storygrid.com/masterwork/tipping-point

SCENE ANALYSIS:

BEGINNING HOOK

INTRODUCTION

SCENE 1

564 words

"For Hush Puppies—the classic ... the space of two years?"

Summary: Hush Puppies shoes went from a brand that was almost dead to one that was thriving.

INQUIRY EVENT

1. Literal Action: What is the author-protagonist literally doing in this scene?

Gladwell introduces the story of how the Hush Puppies brand reached a Tipping Point, exploding in popularity between 1994 and 1995.

2. Essential Action: What is the author trying to accomplish in this scene?

Gladwell wants to raise the question, "Why do certain products or ideas become popular overnight?" by telling the story of the rise in sales of Hush Puppies shoes.

3. Life Value Change: What has changed along the Ignorance to Knowledge to Wisdom spectrum in the scene?

Hush Puppies experiences a rapid growth in sales, changing the external life value from Unpopular to Popular. Gladwell learns the basic facts of the situation but doesn't understand what made the brand tip.
Status Quo Worldview to Cognitive Dissonance

4. Inquiry Event: What is the resulting Inquiry Event?

"How does a thirty-dollar pair of shoes go from a handful of downtown Manhattan hipsters and designers to every mall in America in the space of two years?"

THE FIVE COMMANDMENTS OF STORYTELLING

Inciting Incident: In 1994, Hush Puppies sales were down to 30,000 pairs per year, and it was a dying brand, but in 1995, the brand tipped, selling 430,000 pairs of shoes. What caused the brand to tip?

Progressive Complications: Hush Puppies executives learned that the shoes had become hip in Manhattan and that people were buying the shoes in resale shops and Ma and Pa stores. Manhattan and LA designers wanted the shoes to help sell their products.

The Turning Point Progressive Complication: In 1995, 430,000 pairs of shoes were sold, but company executives didn't know why. The first few kids to wear them were not trying to promote the brand.

Crisis: If the executives don't know why this happened, is there a way to figure it out?

Climax: Gladwell looks at what happened before the brand tipped, but only finds more questions, no definitive answers.

6

Resolution: The brand went from 30,000 to 430,000 pairs sold annually in two years and won a prize in 1996, after a few kids had worn the shoes and designers used them to promote other products. The result was an explosion in popularity in a very short time.

NOTES

- This story contains many of the core ideas that will be introduced later in the book, though they aren't mentioned explicitly: word of mouth, epidemics and contagiousness, the power of small groups, small changes producing big effects, and sudden change.
- The scene explores *what* happened in this illustrative example, but we don't learn exactly *why* it happened. We're still ignorant about the mechanism that caused rapid change for the brand.
- This first example of a Tipping Point is a simple, innocuous business story about a relatable, familiar product that tipped without intention or effort by the executives of the company. It piques our curiosity without being scary.

SCENE 2

495 words
"There was a time, not ... two-thirds in five years?"
Summary: The murder rate and other violent crime dropped dramatically in New York City in a short time in the 1990s.

INQUIRY EVENT

1. Literal Action: What is the author-protagonist literally doing in this scene?

Gladwell introduces the story of violent crime in New York City suddenly dropping within five years.

2. Essential Action: What is the author trying to accomplish with this inquiry event?

Gladwell wants to raise the question, "Why do some dramatic changes in society happen so quickly?" by telling the story of a dramatic change in the crime rate in New York City.

3. Life Value Change: What has changed along the Ignorance to Knowledge to Wisdom spectrum in the scene?

New York City crime plummets, changing the external life value from Dangerous to Safe. But Gladwell doesn't understand the Tipping Point connection yet.
Status Quo Worldview to Cognitive Dissonance

4. Inquiry Event: What is the resulting Inquiry Event?

"How can a change in a handful of economic and social indices cause murder rates to fall by two-thirds in five years?"

THE FIVE COMMANDMENTS OF STORYTELLING

Inciting Incident: In the 1990s, violent crime in poor neighborhoods in New York City dropped dramatically. What accounts for this change?

Progressive Complications: Police say policing strategy improved crime rates. Criminologists say a decline in the crack trade and an aging population explains the change. Economists say the economy improved and led to more jobs and less crime.

The Turning Point Progressive Complication: None of the answers experts provided explain why crime dropped so sharply.

Crisis Question: If experts can't say what caused the change, is there a way to find out?

Climax: To learn why the crime rate dropped in New York City, Gladwell must look further. The Research Knowledge does not provide him with the Higher Knowledge he wants.

Resolution: Violent crime in New York City dropped dramatically in the 1990s, but Gladwell is still left with the question, "How can a change in a handful of economic and social indices cause murder rates to fall by two-thirds in five years?"

NOTES

- The first two scenes establish the phenomenon (obligatory scene) that Gladwell studies in his Big Idea book. We don't yet have definitive explanations for why Hush Puppies rose in popularity and why the crime rate in New York City fell—or what they might have in common, other than extreme and rapid change. Scenes 1 and 2 set up scenes 3 and 4, where the Big Idea is developed and revealed.
- Gladwell hints at the core idea of small changes causing big effects by saying, "There is a puzzling gap between the scale of the changes in policing and the size of the effect on places like Brownsville and East New York."
- Gladwell uses the same sentence in scenes 1 and 2, *"But then something strange happened,"* to signal the change in both situations. This subtle repetition helps connect two drastically different stories about change. He often uses sentences like these to signal an external turning point in a scene.
- In the Hush Puppies example, no one really knows why the shoes grew in popularity. In the New York crime example, different authorities suggest reasons, but these theories, according to Gladwell, turn out to be wrong or at least insufficient to explain the dramatic shift. Social epidemics are confounding, even to the experts, which is one of the lessons of *The Tipping Point* that Gladwell emphasizes in the Ending Payoff. We must test our intuition.

SCENE 3

664 Words
"The Tipping Point is the . . . once is the Tipping Point."
Summary: The Tipping Point is an idea that helps us make sense of a wide variety of swift and dramatic changes.

INQUIRY EVENT

1. Literal Action: What is the author-protagonist literally doing in this scene?

Gladwell looks for a connection between the Hush Puppies and NYC crime stories and actual disease epidemics, such as measles and flu.

2. Essential Action: What is the author-protagonist trying to accomplish in this scene?

Gladwell wants to reveal his big idea and expand it to apply to a wider world of stories beyond Hush Puppies and NYC crime.

3. Life Value Change: What has changed along the Ignorance to Knowledge to Wisdom spectrum in the scene?

Gladwell sums up his worldview journey from initial ignorance to research and shoe-leather knowledge gathered, which turns into wisdom, revealing things to come in later chapters.
Ignorance to Knowledge to Wisdom

4. Inquiry Event: What is the resulting Inquiry Event?

Is it possible that "ideas, messages, behaviors, and products spread just like viruses do"?

THE FIVE COMMANDMENTS OF STORYTELLING

Inciting Incident: Gladwell looks at the accumulated evidence and asks, is there a connection or common thread among mysterious changes that mark everyday life?

Progressive Complications: These changes have three things in common: 1) they are clearly contagious, 2) small changes cause big effects, and 3) they happen quickly, in a dramatic moment.

Turning Point Progressive Complication: The most important aspect of the changes Gladwell is investigating—the thing that may connect them all, he thinks—is that small changes cause big effects.

Crisis Question: Can this idea that small changes cause big results explain "why modern change happens the way it does"?

Climax: Gladwell proposes that a "Tipping Point" could explain modern change.

Resolution: His explanatory model for many big modern changes is called the "Tipping Point."

NOTES

- This is the first full statement of Gladwell's big idea (obligatory scene) and it is incredibly clear and concise: "*The Tipping Point* is the biography of an idea, and the idea is very simple. It is that the best way to understand the emergence of fashion trends, the ebb and flow of crime waves, or, for that matter, the transformation of unknown books into bestsellers, or the rise of teenage smoking, or the phenomena of word of mouth, or any number of the other mysterious changes that mark everyday life is to think of them as epidemics. Ideas and products and messages and behaviors spread just like viruses do."
- Gladwell probably chose the stories of Hush Puppies and the NYC crime rate with purpose because they are positive examples, but they operate in very different realms— fashion and crime—which hints at the vast scope of things to which his Big Idea will apply.

SCENE 4

1548 Words
"A world that follows the ... positive epidemics of our own?"
Summary: Very big and very fast changes (geometric progression) happen in many realms, from "white flight" to the adoption of new technology, and these changes follow many of the rules of epidemics.

INQUIRY EVENT

1. **Literal Action: What is the author-protagonist literally doing in this scene?**

Gladwell describes more examples of big, rapid changes that are recognizable to many readers, and tells us they follow rules of epidemics: contagiousness, small changes lead to big effects, and sudden change.

2. **Essential Action: What is the author-protagonist trying to accomplish in this scene?**

Gladwell wants to persuade readers to accept his hypothesis that rapid social change follows the rules of epidemics and Tipping Points as true and pervasive, not limited to a few examples.

3. Life Value Change: What has changed along the Ignorance to Knowledge to Wisdom spectrum in the scene?

The examples in the scene (yawning, white flight, adoption of fax machines, neighborhood decline) show change spreading quickly and dramatically, changing the external life value from Stasis to Spreading. Gladwell learns that in all these examples—although it's hard to believe at first—change happens all at once with a Tipping Point.
Cognitive Dissonance to Research Knowledge

4. Inquiry Event: What is the resulting Inquiry Event?

Why is it that change often happens dramatically, all at once, not incrementally, and is the "Tipping Point" the key moment of critical mass when that change begins?

THE FIVE COMMANDMENTS OF STORYTELLING

Inciting Incident: Gladwell wonders about the contagiousness of ideas and behaviors that might behave like the flu or epidemics. Can the Tipping Point explain these examples?

Progressive Complications: Ideas, behaviors, and products—from yawning to white flight—can be contagious in multiple and unexpected ways.

The Turning Point Progressive Complication: Dramatic social change, including white flight and adoption of fax machines and cell phones, often happens geometrically (as in his simple paper folding example).

Crisis Question: Gladwell wonders if he can apply Tipping Points to more complex social issues, like neighborhood decline?

Climax: Yes. He uses the research of sociologist Jonathan Crane as proof that he can.

Resolution: Gladwell recaps his understanding of rapid, radical change with the story of his dog and snow, arguing that radical change is not just a possibility, but a certainty (like the weather!).

NOTES

- Gladwell's final sentences in this scene provide two key questions for later. He says: *The point of all of this is to answer two simple questions that lie at the heart of what we would all like to accomplish as educators, parents, marketers, businesspeople, and policy makers. [Nice big market of people who can get something out of this book, eh?] Why is it that some ideas or behaviors or products start epidemics and others don't? And what can we do to deliberately start and control positive epidemics of our own? (alluding to the how-to convention)*. Ending his Beginning Hook with two questions and an emphasis on positive Tipping Points are strong choices that make readers want to keep reading for more answers.
- To make his argument in support of the Big Idea, Gladwell needs us to challenge our intuition about rapid change. In this scene, he presents examples to break down our preconceived notions. We must see rapid change through new eyes if we're going to understand it. This is a critical element of "analyzing" the problem or phenomenon, the work of the Beginning Hook. This scene also sets up part of Gladwell's "mechanization," or how-to, presented in the Ending Payoff. We must test our intuition.
- In the opening line of this scene, "A world that follows the rules of epidemics is a very different place from the world

we think we live in now," Gladwell first establishes the villain, a convention of the external Action-Adventure genre. Remember we said the villain is the human condition, including ignorance and weakness. Though we think we understand our world, we understand very little of what creates our experience. Our weapons against this villain include curiosity and the willingness and courage to pursue knowledge that allows us to make wise decisions and become our best selves.

- From the four little scenes of the Beginning Hook, readers get the entire content of the book in a little over three thousand words. The major points and conclusions are there for the taking, but like any great Beginning Hook, those little nuggets promise far more if you make the commitment to keep reading.
- Gladwell also deliberately inserts a funny little story about his dog toward the end of the Beginning Hook before starting the long march through the complex Middle Build. He has hit us with complicated information and teased that he will be applying his big idea to some heavy subjects even beyond crime rates, including difficult social problems. By using the everyday and easily understood phenomenon of snow and a frisky puppy, he lightens the burden before pulling us forward into the core of the book with teasers of future chapters about *Sesame Street* and *Blue's Clues* . . . and syphilis.

SCENE ANALYSIS:

MIDDLE BUILD

CHAPTER 1 - THE THREE RULES OF EPIDEMICS

SCENE 5

1,056 words
"In the mid-1990s, the city ... and the Power of Context."
Summary: In the mid-1990s, a syphilis epidemic occurred in Baltimore.

INQUIRY EVENT

1. Literal Action: What is the author-protagonist literally doing in this scene?

Gladwell tells the story of how Baltimore experienced an epidemic of syphilis in the mid-1990s.

2. Essential Action: What is the author-protagonist trying to accomplish in this scene?

Gladwell wants to show how disease epidemics tip.

3. Life Value Change: What has changed along the Ignorance to Knowledge to Wisdom spectrum in the scene?

Syphilis in Baltimore went from a disease that was under control to one that was spreading in a short period of time, changing the external life value from Containment to Epidemic. Through this example, Gladwell discovers three different and subtle ways epidemics tip.

Ignorance to Research Knowledge

4. Inquiry Event: What is the resulting Inquiry Event?

What caused Baltimore's syphilis problem to tip?

THE FIVE COMMANDMENTS OF STORYTELLING

Inciting Incident: For years before 1995, the syphilis rate in Baltimore was stable. What made it tip?

Progressive Complications: When the syphilis epidemic occurred, the CDC said it happened because of an increase in the crack cocaine problem, STD expert John Zenilman said budget cuts affected medical services in the poor neighborhoods of the city, and leading epidemiologist John Potterat said the destruction of neighborhoods where people who carried the disease lived caused them to move to other parts of the city.

The Turning Point Progressive Complication: Three plausible reasons explain the syphilis epidemic, but none of these reasons involve drastic change, and each one is different.

Crisis Question: Does this example help us understand the way disease epidemics tip in general?

Climax: There is more than one way to tip a disease epidemic, including changes in the *people* who carry the disease, the *disease itself*, and the *environment* or context in which the disease operates.

Resolution: Disease epidemics tip because a change has occurred in one or more of these three areas. Gladwell calls these agents of change the Law of the Few, the Stickiness Factor, and the Power of Context.

NOTES

- In this scene, Gladwell introduces the three rules of Tipping Points in the context of the Baltimore syphilis epidemic in the mid-1990s. In the next three scenes, he shows how each rule operates in the context of disease epidemics (e.g., the flu, AIDS, syphilis, and gonorrhea) and then offers examples of how each rule works in social epidemics too.
- Gladwell provides commentary on the meaning of the events he is describing. Some findings or conclusions are *obvious* or *interesting*, *strange* or *surprising* or not, and may also be *complicated*, *shocking*, or *chilling*. This seems to be a subtle form of persuasion (or Pathos that is derived from the Ethos Gladwell has already established). If statement *X* is obvious to Gladwell, we're not likely to challenge it. Are we? And are we more likely to trust the statement that is complicated because we assume Gladwell is smarter than we are and has done the intellectual heavy lifting? Probably.

SCENE 6

900 words
"When we say that a ... were able to spread HIV."
Summary: Disease epidemics, like gonorrhea and HIV, often tip as a result of the actions of a few exceptional people.

INQUIRY EVENT

1. Literal Action: What is the author-protagonist literally doing in this scene?

Gladwell introduces several examples of disease epidemics that tipped, specifically related to gonorrhea and HIV.

2. Essential Action: What is the author-protagonist trying to accomplish in this scene?

Gladwell wants to show how the Law of the Few operates in disease epidemics and suggest that it operates the same way in social epidemics.

3. Life Value Change: What has changed along the Ignorance to Knowledge to Wisdom spectrum in the scene?

In all the cases cited, a few infected many with deadly diseases, changing the external life value from Infection to Death. Gladwell learns that social epidemics, like the increase in the sales of Hush Puppies, operate the same way disease epidemics do: one or more exceptional people spread the word or disease to many other people.

Ignorance to Research Knowledge to Higher Knowledge

4. Inquiry Event: What is the resulting Inquiry Event?

When it comes to spreading diseases or social epidemics, why is it that "some people matter more than others"?

THE FIVE COMMANDMENTS OF STORYTELLING

Inciting Incident: Gladwell suggests that whether we're talking about diseases or social phenomena, certain people matter more than others. How can that be?

Progressive Complications: The 80/20 Principle says that a small number of people in any given situation do most of the work. Epidemiologist John Potterat found that 168 people caused gonorrhea to tip in Colorado Springs.

The Turning Point Progressive Complication: Small numbers of people can do substantial damage to a large population.

Crisis Question: Can we understand drastic change better by looking at what's special about these few people?

Climax: These people have lives and behaviors that differ drastically from the norm; they go out every night and have more than the average number of sexual partners.

Resolution: Social epidemics work the same way disease epidemics do, a few exceptional people do the majority of the work, but in the case of social epidemics, the people who spread them are more knowledgeable, sociable, energetic, or influential.

NOTES

- Gladwell notes the common elements among people who spread disease epidemics, like McGee, Williams, and Dugas mentioned in this scene, and the Manhattan hipsters who spread the Hush Puppies brand. Both groups also have these elements in common with people like Maggie and Billy G. (scene 47), who are hard core smokers and by their "cool" example encourage teenagers to smoke.

SCENE 7

1,096 words

"In Baltimore, when the city's ... of an impact it makes."

Summary: A flu pandemic arose in 1918, an epidemic of *Pneumocystis carinii pneumonia* (PCP) arose in the 1950s, and Winston filter-tip cigarettes became the best-selling brand in the US.

INQUIRY EVENT

1. Literal Action: What is the author-protagonist literally doing in this scene?

Gladwell tells the stories of three "messages" that changed to become sticky: the 1918 flu pandemic, a 1950s epidemic of PCP, and Winston filter-tip cigarettes.

2. Essential Action: What is the author-protagonist trying to accomplish in this scene?

Gladwell wants to show that for disease epidemics to "stick" and become

33

deadly, they must mutate. He suggests that Stickiness operates the same way in social epidemics, making them more powerful.

3. Life Value Change: What has changed along the Ignorance to Knowledge to Wisdom spectrum in the scene?

Transformations in diseases like the 1918 flu epidemic and early HIV led to millions of deaths in a short time, changing the external life value from Acute to Deadly. By studying these diseases, Gladwell learns that viruses mutate and become more likely to "stick."

Ignorance to Research Knowledge to Higher Knowledge

4. Inquiry Event: What is the resulting Inquiry Event?

How does the Stickiness Factor change viruses and make them more dangerous?

THE FIVE COMMANDMENTS OF STORYTELLING

Inciting Incident: The 1918 flu epidemic began unremarkably. What caused it to become a pandemic?

Progressive Complications: Within six months, twenty to forty million people died. Similarly, PCP was much less deadly in the 1950s than when HIV/AIDS tipped in the 1980s. AIDS researcher Jaap Goudsmit argues that the 1950s PCP outbreak accompanied a different, less deadly form of HIV and that two-thirds of children survived.

The Turning Point Progressive Complication: Changes in the virus or message affect its Stickiness. "Once it infected you, you stayed infected. It stuck."

Crisis Question: How does the Stickiness Factor operate in social epidemics?

Climax: Winston cigarettes adopted a catchy (sticky) slogan and within months, passed several other cigarette brands to become the second most popular in the US.

Resolution: Stickiness is required for a virus or a message to tip, whether for disease or social epidemics: The message must be memorable to be acted upon.

NOTES

- Gladwell makes the point that people focus on how to make an idea contagious, but the challenge is in making the message stick. If the message is forgotten, it will have no impact.
- This scene is an example in which Gladwell may be fairly criticized for making too much of flimsy evidence, especially related to the PCP-AIDS connection. In general, if a writer has a hunch to put forth or is making claims that are not fully supported by the available information, a good policy is to own it. Admit that you're offering an unproven hypothesis. The better policy is to find stronger evidence and illustrations in the first place.

SCENE 8

907 words

"Every time someone in Baltimore ... environment than they may seem."
Summary: The spread of sexually transmitted diseases in Baltimore is affected by the seasons. Kitty Genovese's New York City neighbors did not call the police when they heard her being attacked.

INQUIRY EVENT

1. Literal Action: What is the author-protagonist literally doing in this scene?

Gladwell tells the story of how environmental factors affect the spread of sexually transmitted diseases and introduces the story of Kitty Genovese, who was attacked and killed while thirty-eight neighbors watched without calling the police.

2. Essential Action: What is the author-protagonist trying to accomplish in this scene?

Gladwell wants to show how the Power of Context operates in disease epidemics and suggests it operates the same way in social epidemics.

3. Life Value Change: What has changed along the Ignorance to Knowledge to Wisdom spectrum in the scene?

Kitty Genovese's neighbors observed the attack on her but were not moved to act on her behalf, so the external life value shift is Caring to Uncaring. Gladwell learns that the relevant fact is not that none of the thirty-eight witnesses called the police; it's that no one called precisely because so many people were observing.

Ignorance to Research Knowledge to Higher Knowledge

4. Inquiry Event: What is the resulting Inquiry Event?

What influence does context or environment have on epidemics in general?

THE FIVE COMMANDMENTS OF STORYTELLING

Inciting Incident: Maps showing when and where people seek treatment for sexually transmitted diseases in Baltimore reflect changes in the seasons. How does the environment affect the spread of diseases?

Progressive Complications: In the summer, sexually transmitted diseases spread outward from downtown, but in the winter most cases are limited to two central areas.

The Turning Point Progressive Complication: Changes in the environment have big effects on the spread of disease epidemics.

Crisis Question: Can environmental factors help us understand why Kitty Genovese's neighbors didn't call the police when she was attacked?

Climax: Yes, but not in the way we might think. People often assume it's because of the dehumanizing effects of living in a big city. But the "bystander problem" suggests that it's because when other people are present, we're more likely to assume someone else will take responsibility. Changes in behavior sometimes depend on the smallest of contextual details.

Resolution: The Power of Context shows us that we're a lot more sensitive to our surroundings than we think, and not always in the ways we think, whether we're talking about disease epidemics or social epidemics.

NOTES

- Gladwell really leverages point of view in this scene. He writes, "This is the kind of environmental explanation that makes intuitive sense to us," and he seems to let us off the hook, suggesting we're not stupid (i.e., incapable of understanding) if we initially thought Kitty Genovese died because people in big cities are uncaring. It sounds as if he may have reached the same conclusion. By deploying first person plural, Gladwell makes sure that we readers are in this with him, staying open and curious, and capable of gaining knowledge.
- Later in the scene, he steps back into third person when he writes, "The Power of Context says that human beings are a lot more sensitive to their environment than they may seem."
- Gladwell returns to the idea that the size of a group changes the environment and affects our behavior in scenes 35-38 in the context of best-selling novels, religious movements, and corporations.

SCENE 9

97 words

"The three rules of the ... The answers may surprise you."

Summary: The three rules of Tipping Points are the Law of the Few, the Stickiness Factor, and the Power of Context.

INQUIRY EVENT

1. Literal Action: What is the author-protagonist literally doing in this scene?

Gladwell recaps the three rules of Tipping Points and tells us where the book goes from this point.

2. Essential Action: What is the author-protagonist trying to accomplish in this scene?

Gladwell wants to recap ("tell them what you told them"), but he also wants the reader to keep reading, so he reveals coming attractions.

3. Life Value Change: What has changed along the Ignorance to Knowledge to Wisdom spectrum in the scene?

Because this is a recap of previous stories, there is no critical external value shift. Gladwell learns the three rules of Tipping Points, gaining a new understanding of why Hush Puppies started selling and why crime dropped in New York City.

Status Quo Worldview to Ignorance to Knowledge

4. Inquiry Event: What is the resulting Inquiry Event?

Can the three rules established so far help us understand other puzzling situations?

THE FIVE COMMANDMENTS OF STORYTELLING

Inciting Incident: The three rules of Tipping Points help us make sense of epidemics. Can we use this knowledge of the three rules to gain wisdom about rapid drastic change in the modern world?

Progressive Complications: N/A

The Turning Point Progressive Complication: The three rules of Tipping Points explain the examples Gladwell has explored so far.

Crisis Question: Can the rules help us understand teenage smoking, word of mouth, crime, or the rise of a bestseller?

Climax: The surprising answers come in the pages that follow.

Resolution: We can test the rules of Tipping Points in other situations to see if they can explain a broader range of situations.

NOTES

- Gladwell has now completed the first part of formalizing his analysis. At this point, Gladwell has given us the goods. We know the three rules of Tipping Points, and we've seen how they apply to disease epidemics and social epidemics. We could put the book down now, but he promises to help us understand other phenomena, "teenage smoking, for example, or the phenomenon of word of mouth, or crime, or the rise of a bestseller." Then he suggests there is more to learn because the way the three rules apply to these examples "may surprise you." (narrative cliffhanger convention)
- In the spreadsheet, the Core Stories Cited column sometimes includes stories from prior scenes and sometimes stories from later scenes. This shows how Gladwell foreshadows stories to come and reminds us of stories he's already shared that support his Big Idea, providing continuity throughout the book.

CHAPTER 2 - THE LAW OF THE FEW

SCENE 10

1072 words

"On the afternoon of April ... them Connectors, Mavens, and Salesmen."

Summary: In 1775, Paul Revere rode at night to rouse the militia in the towns around Boston to fight the British.

INQUIRY EVENT

1. Literal Action: What is the author-protagonist literally doing in this scene?

Gladwell tells the story of Paul Revere, who warns villagers on the outskirts of Boston that the British are about to attack. People heed Revere's warnings but ignore William Dawes, another man who did the same thing at the same time.

2. Essential Action: What is the author-protagonist trying to accomplish in this scene?

Gladwell wants to show that certain types of people are critical to the spread of messages, introducing the concepts of Connectors, Mavens, and Salespeople.

3. Life Value Change: What has changed along the Ignorance to Knowledge to Wisdom spectrum in the scene?

Paul Revere's actions informed many villagers that the British were coming, changing the external life value from Unprepared to Prepared. Gladwell learns that Revere's message spread better than Dawes's message, but he doesn't know exactly why.

Status Quo Worldview to Cognitive Dissonance

4. Inquiry Event: What is the resulting Inquiry Event?

Why do some ideas, trends, and pieces of news "tip" and become viral, but others don't?

THE FIVE COMMANDMENTS OF STORYTELLING

Inciting Incident: News of a possible impending British attack reaches Paul Revere and William Dawes. Will the men be able to help defend their neighbors?

Progressive Complications: Revere compares notes with his friend Joseph Warren, and they decide the evidence points to an attack on Lexington and Concord, so the surrounding towns must be warned. William Dawes makes the same decision.

The Turning Point Progressive Complication: Revere rides to many small towns around Boston, warning people of the impending attack. This information spreads like a virus, but Dawes's identical message didn't spread.

Crisis Question: Do characteristics of the two men account for the difference?

Climax: Gladwell believes Revere's success must be due to some special gifts, but he does not yet understand what those gifts are.

Resolution: The story sparks Gladwell's curiosity about Connectors, Mavens, and Salespeople.

NOTES

- Gladwell combines a well-known historical event—Paul Revere's ride—with a highly personal side anecdote about restaurants in his neighborhood to highlight the question he's going to tackle in the chapter. He frequently adds personal stories to the core stories he is investigating, which allows him to bring the analysis down to a more mundane level that will feel familiar to any reader and also allows him to mix third- and first-person points of view.
- Gladwell refers to the Stickiness Factor of the message of Paul Revere without explicitly mentioning it.
- This scene is an example of a narrative cliffhanger, one of the conventions of Big Idea nonfiction. Gladwell tells us that the Law of the Few explains why Revere's message tipped while Dawes's did not, but he doesn't yet reveal what qualities Revere possessed that Dawes did not.

SCENE 11

1326 words

"In the late 1960s, the . . . for bringing the world together."
Summary: Psychologist Stanley Milgram traced how information traveled from 160 people in Omaha, Nebraska, to one person in Sharon, Massachusetts, discovering that on average it took only five steps.

INQUIRY EVENT

1. Literal Action: What is the author-protagonist literally doing in this scene?

Gladwell introduces the concept of Connectors, combining the research of three psychology studies with an illustration based on his own group of friends to show how Connectors work.

2. Essential Action: What is the author-protagonist trying to accomplish in this scene?

Gladwell wants to demonstrate that a particular type of person, called a

Connector, with "a special gift for bringing the world together," is essential to the viral spread of information.

3. Life Value Change: What has changed along the Ignorance to Knowledge to Wisdom spectrum in the scene?

During the course of the experiment, people in Omaha and Massachusetts become clearly linked, changing the external life value from Unconnected to Connected. Gladwell gains knowledge by studying the experiment, learning that a large disparate group of people in one place has traceable links to one person in another place. He begins to understand how Connectors work, that connections are formed at hubs, and that he can apply this knowledge to other situations.

Ignorance to Research Knowledge to Higher Knowledge

4. Inquiry Event: What is the resulting Inquiry Event?

Is the spread of information, ideas, and trends helped by the fact that human beings are intimately linked through special individuals who act as Connectors?

THE FIVE COMMANDMENTS OF STORYTELLING

Inciting Incident: Psychologist Stanley Milgram asked 160 people in Omaha to get a packet of information to a stockbroker in Massachusetts in order to investigate long-distance connections. How many connections will it take?

Progressive Complications: The Omahans used various routes via friends, acquaintances, and relatives to reach the stockbroker. Milgram tracked the progress of each packet through these routes.

The Turning Point Progressive Complication: Half the letters reached their destination through just three key people, and in other cases only five or six people were needed, sparking Gladwell to wonder about those key people.

Crisis Question: Is there an explanation for why so few steps/so few people are needed?

Climax: Yes. Some people operate in the world as Connectors, specializing in linking many others to the rest of the world.

Resolution: Gladwell realizes he has a Connector in his own life, Jacob Weisberg, and this realization solidifies the meaning and power of Connectors for him.

NOTES

- Gladwell is meticulous in reminding readers how all his disparate stories are connected. In a chapter primarily devoted to the "six degrees of separation" story, he circles back to include examples from Paul Revere's ride and Hush Puppies toward the end. The secondary stories, including a story about the author's own personal friendships, support the truth of the primary story. This is an important lesson for writers of any Big Idea nonfiction book.

SCENE 12

2312 words

"What makes someone a Connector? ... one human being from another."

Summary: A phone book test helps to estimate the number of friends and acquaintances a person has. True Connectors "collect people the way others collect stamps."

INQUIRY EVENT

1. Literal Action: What is the author-protagonist literally doing in this scene?

Gladwell meets and tells readers all about Roger Horchow, an extraordinary Connector, who becomes one of the author's essential sidekicks. (Shawn Coyne calls him a scarecrow, referring to the iconic sidekick on Dorothy's journey in The Wizard of Oz.*)*

2. Essential Action: What is the author-protagonist trying to accomplish in this scene?

Gladwell wants to understand what makes Connectors special, but he

55

doesn't come away with definite answers, only identifying a general Connector "impulse" by talking with Horchow.

3. Life Value Change: What has changed along the Ignorance to Knowledge to Wisdom spectrum in the scene?

Horchow becomes a sidekick, changing Gladwell's own external life value from Alone to Partnered. Gladwell gathers important new information from conversations with Horchow, including the understanding that Connectors form weak ties.
Ignorance to Shoe-Leather Knowledge

4. Inquiry Event: What is the resulting Inquiry Event?

What qualities make someone a great Connector?

THE FIVE COMMANDMENTS OF STORYTELLING

Inciting Incident: Gladwell meets Roger Horchow through his daughter, a friend of Gladwell, and is instantly intrigued. What are Horchow's Connector characteristics?

Progressive Complications: Gladwell listens to Horchow's many stories and gives him the phone book test.

The Turning Point Progressive Complication: Horchow scores a 98 on the phone book test, and Gladwell now recognizes the importance of high numbers of acquaintances in identifying a Connector.

Crisis Question: Will Gladwell ever be able to understand exactly what makes Horchow a great Connector?

Climax: Yes. Gladwell learns that Horchow's success as a Connector is a result of "weak ties," friendly but casual social connections.

Resolution: Gladwell understands Connectors on a deeper level. They have an impulse toward weak ties that enables them to collect a high number of acquaintances.

NOTES

- This scene begins unusually, with an explicit statement of the inquiry event. This choice is helpful for readers.
- Part of the purpose of the scene is to foreshadow the Rule of 150 that will appear later in the book. And one of the great things about the scene is that its form follows its function. Gladwell is investigating people who are connected to extraordinarily large numbers of other people, and in this chapter, he mentions more people's names than in any other!

SCENE 13

2059 words

"Connectors are important for more ... and Roger like them all."

Summary: Academic research and Gladwell's friend group both demonstrate that people who move among many different worlds are ideal Connectors.

INQUIRY EVENT

1. Literal Action: What is the author-protagonist literally doing in this scene?

Gladwell tells two stories: One about the research of Brett Tjaden into the Six Degrees of Kevin Bacon game; and the other, the story of Lois Weisberg, a woman with many careers and friendships in Chicago from the 1950s to the present. He uses Tjaden's research and Weisberg's life to analyze Connectors.

2. Essential Action: What is the author-protagonist trying to accomplish in this scene?

Gladwell wants to improve his theory of the importance of Connectors with a demonstration of exactly how they work. With "a foot in so many different worlds, they have the effect of bringing them all together."

3. Life Value Change: What has changed along the Ignorance to Knowledge to Wisdom spectrum in the scene?

Lois Weisberg becomes a sidekick (Shawn Coyne calls her the "tin man") on Gladwell's journey, changing Gladwell's external life value from Unconnected to Connected. From Weisberg and Tjaden he learns that Connectors span many different worlds, amassing a lot of knowledge about those worlds.

Ignorance to Research and Shoe-Leather Knowledge to Higher Knowledge

4. Inquiry Event: What is the resulting Inquiry Event?

Do great Connectors depend on not only the number of their acquaintances, but also certain qualities of those acquaintances?

THE FIVE COMMANDMENTS OF STORYTELLING

Inciting Incident: Gladwell learns that computer scientist Brett Tjaden has analyzed the average number of steps actors and actresses are separated from Kevin Bacon, and discovered it's 2.8. Is there more to it than numbers?

Progressive Complications: The data shows that actors like Rod Steiger, who moves among many different types of roles, are the best connected.

The Turning Point Progressive Complication: Through Tjaden, Gladwell realizes it's not just the number of people a Connector knows. The diversity of the connections matter.

Crisis Question: Can Gladwell identify qualities that define great Connectors?

Climax: Yes, he finds the classic Connector qualities in Lois Weisberg.

Resolution: Gladwell shows that Lois Weisberg and other great Connectors have an instinct that helps them relate to people they meet. It's more than just living in diverse worlds; it's the fact that people like Weisberg and Horchow see possibility in other people and "like them all."

NOTES

- Readers who are paying attention will notice that Lois Weisberg, the super Connector, and Jacob Weisberg, Gladwell's Connector best friend, are related—raising the question of whether being a Connector is an inherited trait.

SCENE 14

676 words

"There is a very good ... a person like Roger Horchow."

Summary: A sociologist's studies reveal the importance of occasional, or weak, personal contacts in the job-hunting process, prompting more questions about Connectors.

INQUIRY EVENT

1. Literal Action: What is the author-protagonist literally doing in this scene?

Gladwell examines the work of sociologist Mark Granovetter, which reveals that weak personal ties are the most likely way of spreading information (about jobs, in this case). Gladwell applies this insight to other word-of-mouth phenomena with a story about restaurant recommendations.

2. Essential Action: What is the author-protagonist trying to accomplish in this scene?

Gladwell wants to link several ideas and stories already discussed in order to deepen his understanding of how word of mouth works.

3. Life Value Change: What has changed along the Ignorance to Knowledge to Wisdom spectrum in the scene?

Gladwell learns from Granovetter's research about the value of acquaintances in job searches and in spreading information (restaurant reviews), changing the external life value of the job seekers and restaurants from Undiscovered to Familiar. But he also deepens his understanding by realizing that weak ties are better for expanding connections.

Cognitive Dissonance to Shoe-Leather and Research Knowledge to Higher Knowledge

4. Inquiry Event: What is the resulting Inquiry Event?

Is it possible that weak ties are more important in the spread of ideas, trends, and information via word of mouth than strong ties?

THE FIVE COMMANDMENTS OF STORYTELLING

Inciting Incident: Gladwell looks at the work of sociologist Mark Granovetter, who studies data about job seekers, and finds new information about Connectors in job searches. He wonders why casual, weak ties are so valuable?

Progressive Complications: Granovetter's statistics show workers are more likely to find jobs via "occasional" personal contacts, not close friends.

The Turning Point Progressive Complication: Gladwell experiences a moment of Cognitive Dissonance. It's not friends who help people get jobs, it's acquaintances? That's counterintuitive.

Crisis Question: Is there an explanation for why friends don't work as well as Connectors?

Climax: Yes, acquaintances are more likely to know something you don't while friends usually occupy the same world as you do, so they can't reach across worlds.

Resolution: Gladwell learns a story from Horchow's daughter that confirms his new understanding about the importance of weak ties in the spread of ideas, trends, and information.

NOTES

- This small scene and a small moment of Cognitive Dissonance allow Gladwell to bring readers with him as he ties several strands of the story together. He creates a "principle," describing weak ties as the key to the movement of ideas and mentioning Hush Puppies again as an example, to cement the principle in readers' minds.
- Because he emphasizes how counterintuitive some of the new information is, this is also a moment when Gladwell briefly wrestles with the book's antagonist or "villain" of human ignorance.

SCENE 15

832 words

"Here, then, is the explanation ... was just an ordinary man."

Summary: The story of Paul Revere returns to center stage but looks different with the new insight about what makes a word-of-mouth epidemic happen.

INQUIRY EVENT

1. Literal Action: What is the author-protagonist literally doing in this scene?

Gladwell retells the story of Paul Revere from earlier in the book (scene 10), in light of his new wisdom about Connectors.

2. Essential Action: What is the author-protagonist trying to accomplish in this scene?

Providing more details about the characteristics of Paul Revere and William Dawes, Gladwell wants to demonstrate that Revere was a true

Connector and Dawes was "just an ordinary man," which explains why Revere's ride was successful and Dawes's was not.

3. Life Value Change: What has changed along the Ignorance to Knowledge to Wisdom spectrum in the scene?

Many qualities made Revere a Connector, moving his external life value from Ordinary to Super Connected. Gladwell is able to synthesize all the knowledge he has amassed and apply it to an earlier puzzle directly related to his Big Idea.

Research and Shoe-Leather Knowledge to Higher Knowledge to Wisdom

4. Inquiry Event: What is the resulting Inquiry Event?

Did Paul Revere succeed in his word-of-mouth mission because he had all the characteristics of a true Connector?

THE FIVE COMMANDMENTS OF STORYTELLING

Inciting Incident: Gladwell learns more about Paul Revere's personality by reading David Hackett Fischer's book about him. Can Revere's specific characteristics reveal more about the power of Connectors?

Progressive Complications: Gladwell learns about Revere's success as a fisherman and hunter, cardplayer and theater-lover, regular at the pubs, businessman, member of many clubs, etc.

The Turning Point Progressive Complication: Gladwell realizes that Revere "knew everybody," had plenty of weak ties, and was "naturally and irrepressibly social," making him the perfect Connector.

Crisis Question: Can the concept of Connectors explain the difference between Revere and Dawes?

Climax: Yes, Revere was a link among many far-flung groups, and was a Revolutionary Era version of Weisberg and Horchow.

Resolution: Gladwell's understanding of the power of Connectors is proven right by showing the evidence of that theory in the case of Revere and Dawes.

NOTES

- Writers should note that it's helpful to readers and to your own argument to circle back to a previous story—as Gladwell does here with Paul Revere—to apply a new concept before moving on in your analysis.

SCENE 16

1219 words

"It would be a mistake ... His name is Mark Alpert."

Summary: Scholar Linda Price has a lot of insights to share about information specialists called Mavens.

INQUIRY EVENT

1. Literal Action: What is the author-protagonist literally doing in this scene?

Gladwell senses there is another key person in the dissemination of word-of-mouth epidemics. He looks at his research on Paul Revere and talks with new sidekick Linda Price to understand the definition of "the Maven." This is the start of a new journey.

2. Essential Action: What is the author-protagonist trying to accomplish in this scene?

Gladwell wants to find out if Mavens are as critical to social epidemics as Connectors, but he must first understand exactly what they do.

3. Life Value Change: What has changed along the Ignorance to Knowledge to Wisdom spectrum in the scene?

Linda Price schools Gladwell on the lives of Mavens. In terms of Gladwell's larger journey, this is a pure knowledge-gathering scene.
Ignorance to Research and Shoe-Leather Knowledge

4. Inquiry Event: What is the resulting Inquiry Event?

Who provides Connectors with the information they are sharing?

THE FIVE COMMANDMENTS OF STORYTELLING

Inciting Incident: Gladwell realizes a piece is missing from all his stories if he doesn't know how Connectors get the key information they are spreading. Can he figure out the sources?

Progressive Complications: Gladwell wonders: Who told Horchow about the restaurant? Who told the style Connectors about Hush Puppies? How did Revere know so much about the British military?

The Turning Point Progressive Complication: Gladwell realizes there are two kinds of specialists: people specialists (Connectors) and information specialists (Mavens).

Crisis Question: Can Gladwell understand what makes a Maven a Maven?

Climax: Yes, he learns the ways of the Maven from Linda Price, including how detail-obsessed they are and that "they like to be helpers in the marketplace . . . They are socially motivated."

Resolution: Linda Price sends Gladwell to see a super Maven, Mark Alpert.

NOTES

- In this scene, Gladwell provides the first hint that understanding Tipping Points may have negative applications. In discussing Everyday Low Prices, he says, "This is, when you think about it, a potentially disturbing piece of information."
- The reader may wonder whether Gladwell sees himself as a modern Paul Revere—an information specialist and a people specialist. And is he writing this book as a warning to rouse a sleeping population too?

SCENE 17

1119 words

"Mark Alpert is a slender ... makes the American system great."

Summary: Gladwell has lunch with Mark Alpert and learns what being a Maven is all about.

INQUIRY EVENT

1. Literal Action: What is the author-protagonist literally doing in this scene?

Gladwell analyzes Mark Alpert's life as a Maven.

2. Essential Action: What is the author-protagonist trying to accomplish in this scene?

Gladwell wants to understand and illustrate some key characteristics of Mavens via Alpert's life and obsessions.

3. Life Value Change: What has changed along the Ignorance to Knowledge to Wisdom spectrum in the scene?

75

A story-within-a-story that Alpert relates to Gladwell includes an external life value shift from Sharing to Withholding. Gladwell deepens his understanding of Mavens by talking with Alpert and applies this to his larger understanding of Tipping Points.

Ignorance to Shoe-Leather Knowledge to Higher Knowledge

4. Inquiry Event: What is the resulting Inquiry Event?

What role does helping others play in the motivation of Mavens to share so much information?

THE FIVE COMMANDMENTS OF STORYTELLING

Inciting Incident: Gladwell and Alpert meet at an Austin restaurant. Will talking with Alpert reveal new insights about Mavens?

Progressive Complications: Alpert insists on changing tables, explains the value of cable TV, discusses Leonard Maltin's movie guide, tells Gladwell how to get a hotel deal and why he should not buy an Audi, and more!

The Turning Point Progressive Complication: Alpert shares a story about being next to a kid in a supermarket who is buying cigarettes and wanting to dissuade him.

Crisis Question: Will Alpert tell the kid he has lung cancer?

Climax: No. Alpert does not tell the kid about his diagnosis.

Resolution: The story-within-a-story reveals to Gladwell that Mavens are sincere in wanting to help others. This is one of their core characteristics, but Alpert is also self-aware enough to hold back: "I try to be a very passive Maven."

NOTES

- This scene brings some lightness and levity to the book, with a charming character who is able to laugh at himself, yet also slyly mentions one of the more serious topics that will feature so prominently in the rest of the book—teen smoking.

SCENE 18

748 words

"What makes people like Mark . . . spark word-of-mouth epidemics."

Summary: Mark Alpert gives Gladwell advice on where to stay on a visit to Los Angeles, which sparks some thoughts about epidemics!

INQUIRY EVENT

1. Literal Action: What is the author-protagonist literally doing in this scene?

Gladwell analyzes the power of Mavens in spreading information.

2. Essential Action: What is the author-protagonist trying to accomplish in this scene?

Gladwell wants to illustrate in a microcosm why Mavens are so important in starting or spreading epidemics.

3. Life Value Change: What has changed along the Ignorance to Knowledge to Wisdom spectrum in the scene?

Gladwell, in effect, starts a small word-of-mouth epidemic, shifting the life value of those involved from Inexperienced to Savvy. In taking on the role of Connector himself, he learns another lesson about Mavens.

Ignorance to Shoe-Leather Knowledge to Higher Knowledge

4. Inquiry Event: What is the resulting Inquiry Event?

What makes Mavens so important in spreading word-of-mouth epidemics? What role does the authenticity of their information play?

THE FIVE COMMANDMENTS OF STORYTELLING

Inciting Incident: Gladwell tells Alpert he will be going to Los Angeles soon and gets some hotel advice. What happens when he follows the advice?

Progressive Complications: Alpert recommends a hotel, enthuses about its advantages, and convinces Gladwell to stay there.

The Turning Point Progressive Complication: Gladwell is so delighted with the hotel that he recommends it to friends, becoming a Connector and Maven himself.

Crisis Question: Would people more likely follow Alpert's advice or Horchow's? Who's the better epidemic-spreader?

Climax: More would follow Alpert's advice because of his sincerity and enthusiasm, but Horchow would have contact with more people to whom he could give the recommendation.

Resolution: Gladwell deepens his understanding of social epidemics. He understands two types of people spread word-of-mouth epidemics in very different ways.

NOTES

- This story subtly introduces the idea that simple helpfulness and generosity, with no agenda, is "an awfully effective way of getting someone's attention." Gladwell connects that spirit of generosity to both the Hush Puppies and the Paul Revere stories.
- A lesson for writers in Gladwell's interaction with Alpert is that it's important sometimes to become a participant in the events you are reporting to gain a new perspective. This is one way traditional journalism (which tends to emphasize keeping the reporter out of the story) and Big Idea books differ.

SCENE 19

1402 words
"The one thing that a ... don't try, you'll never succeed."
Summary: Tom Gau shows off his qualities as a Salesperson.

INQUIRY EVENT

1. Literal Action: What is the author-protagonist literally doing in this scene?

Gladwell investigates the qualities of a great Salesperson by talking with Tom Gau.

2. Essential Action: What is the author-protagonist trying to accomplish in this scene?

Gladwell wants to distinguish the traits of a great persuader or Salesperson from those of Connectors and Mavens.

3. Life Value Change: What has changed along the Ignorance to Knowledge to Wisdom spectrum in the scene?

83

Gladwell meets and is won over by Gau, who possesses energy, enthusiasm, and charm, changing the external life value from Skeptical to Persuaded (of the power of optimism). Gladwell learns that true Salespeople persuade others to make an active change.

Ignorance to Shoe-Leather Knowledge

4. Inquiry Event: What is the resulting Inquiry Event?

What are the characteristics of the third essential group involved in spreading epidemics, the Salespeople?

THE FIVE COMMANDMENTS OF STORYTELLING

Inciting Incident: Donald Moine introduces Gladwell to Tom Gau, a financial planner. What characteristics make him a good Salesperson?

Progressive Complications: Gau floods Gladwell with statements and questions that reveal his personal characteristics.

The Turning Point Progressive Complication: Gau demonstrates the qualities that make him a great Salesperson: energy, enthusiasm, charm, and likability.

Crisis Question: Will Gau get the house he made an offer on? Are his powers of persuasion that strong?

Climax: Yes, he will get the house.

Resolution: Gladwell understands that a key characteristic of Salespeople is optimism and is persuaded that it works.

NOTES

- Gladwell lets Gau's own flood of words dominate the second half of the chapter. The Salesperson's own energetic, enthusiastic, and optimistic voice is the perfect evidence of the characteristics Gladwell is trying to define. A wonderful lesson for writers: Let your characters do some of the heavy lifting.
- Gladwell offers up short, sharp, memorable descriptions to review his three types of people. Mavens are data banks. Connectors are social glue. Salespeople are persuaders.

SCENE 20

1736 words

"The question of what makes . . . the hidden, and the unspoken."

Summary: Two academic studies about persuasion reveal its subtleties:
1) little things can make a big difference, 2) nonverbal cues are as
important as verbal cues, 3) persuasion works in ways we do not always
appreciate.

INQUIRY EVENT

**1. Literal Action: What is the author-protagonist literally doing in
this scene?**

*Gladwell analyzes two scientific studies. One examines subtle forms of
persuasion in newscasters, and the other examines the persuasive power of
nonverbal actions in students.*

**2. Essential Action: What is the author-protagonist trying to
accomplish in this scene?**

Gladwell wants to draw more general conclusions about what makes someone or something persuasive.

3. Life Value Change: What has changed along the Ignorance to Knowledge to Wisdom spectrum in the scene?

People who watched Peter Jennings's news reports in 1984, in which Jennings smiled when discussing candidate Ronald Reagan, were more likely to vote for Reagan. Students who nodded while listening to editorials advocating an increase in tuition ended up favoring increased tuition. In both cases the life value shifted from Undecided to Persuaded. From both experiments, Gladwell learns that persuasion is nonverbal.
Ignorance to Research Knowledge

4. Inquiry Event: What is the resulting Inquiry Event?

How do nonverbal actions—including smiles, frowns, and nods—contribute to the process of persuasion?

THE FIVE COMMANDMENTS OF STORYTELLING

Inciting Incident: An experiment in 1984 demonstrated that Peter Jennings's subtle pro-Reagan bias affected viewers' voting. What is the power of nonverbal persuasion in other contexts?

Progressive Complications: Another experiment demonstrated that nonverbal actions (head movements) affected students' opinions of tuition increases, even counteracting their own self-interest.

The Turning Point Progressive Complication: Gladwell combines evidence from two studies to come up with three conclusions about the nature of persuasion.

Crisis Question: Can people be persuaded by things that are arbitrary and subtle, such as smiles and nods?

Climax: Yes, they certainly can, according to this evidence.

Resolution: To understand the power of persuaders or Salespeople one must look at "the subtle, the hidden, and the unspoken."

NOTES

- A second negative aspect of Tipping Points emerges in this chapter. Gladwell notes that persuasion in newscasts is subtle and therefore difficult to protect ourselves against. He suggests that companies could perhaps make their TV ads even more effective by using visual cues to force viewers to nod their heads up and down.
- This is an important chapter in which Gladwell moves from individual bits of research toward the more universal arguments he will make about Tipping Points. However, readers may wonder whether these two small studies are fairly weak evidence on which to build larger points.

SCENE 21

2155 words

"What happens when two people ... 117 points, he scored 116."

Summary: An academic study of micromovements reveals new details about Tom Gau's powers as a Salesperson.

INQUIRY EVENT

1. Literal Action: What is the author-protagonist literally doing in this scene?

Gladwell analyzes his earlier visit with Tom Gau in light of research about charisma, micro movements, and persuasion, coming to some deeper and perhaps darker conclusions than before.

2. Essential Action: What is the author-protagonist trying to accomplish in this scene?

Gladwell wants to demonstrate that emotion is truly contagious and show how that works via microrhythms of communication.

3. Life Value Change: What has changed along the Ignorance to Knowledge to Wisdom spectrum in the scene?

After reviewing some studies of the subtle power of movement in communication, Gladwell observes that his conversation with Gau was "conducted on his terms, not mine," with Gau establishing his control quickly and nonverbally, changing the external life value from Disinterested to Seduced. Gladwell puts together his experiences with Gau and several of the studies he's discussed to come to the understanding that dominant personalities persuade through emotion and charisma.

Research and Shoe-Leather Knowledge to Higher Knowledge

4. Inquiry Event: What is the resulting Inquiry Event?

How do charismatic people "infect" others with emotions, an important step on the road to viral dissemination of ideas?

THE FIVE COMMANDMENTS OF STORYTELLING

Inciting Incident: Gladwell re-examines his visit to Gau's office. What is the power of persuasion all about?

Progressive Complications: Gladwell notes all the external elements and then analyzes his interaction with Gau in light of William Condon's decoding of four and a half seconds of film to study micro movements during conversation.

The Turning Point Progressive Complication: Gladwell sees that he was drawn into Gau's emotional rhythms and seduced.

Crisis Question: Do the persuasive, seductive powers Gladwell discovered apply to all Salespeople?

Climax: Yes, Gladwell finds that the essence of Salespeople is that they cannot be resisted; their persuasive powers prey on emotions at a nonverbal level.

Resolution: The new idea of an emotional contagion, with some people as senders and some as receivers, is solidified for Gladwell with a final look at Tom Gau and the charisma test.

NOTES

- Gladwell is moving much further toward negative terminology in this chapter, using "infect" to describe the way Salespeople persuade people.

SCENE 22

414 words

"In the early hours of ... a Maven and a Connector."

Summary: The Paul Revere story looks different in light of all the iconic character types investigated: Maven, Connector, Salesperson.

INQUIRY EVENT

1. Literal Action: What is the author-protagonist literally doing in this scene?

Gladwell re-examines the American colonists defending themselves against British Regulars at Lexington and Concord in April of 1775 in a more extended version of the story he told in previous scenes. They are defeated at Lexington, but the success of Paul Revere leads to a victory for the militia at Concord.

2. Essential Action: What is the author-protagonist trying to accomplish in this scene?

Gladwell wants to take the research in previous scenes to a deeper level to

95

show that Paul Revere's success depended on his skills as a Maven and Connector, and his ability to enlist Salespeople to the cause.

3. Life Value Change: What has changed along the Ignorance to Knowledge to Wisdom spectrum in the scene?

The colonists revolt and defeat the British because of Paul Revere's message, changing the external life value from Subjugated to Resisting. Gladwell concludes that Paul Revere's success was a result of the way he spread his message.

Higher Knowledge to Wisdom

4. Inquiry Event: What is the resulting Inquiry Event?

Can we view the events and characters involved in the Battle of Lexington and Concord in a new and better way in light of our understanding of Mavens, Connectors, and Salespeople as part of the process of spreading a social "epidemic" or message?

THE FIVE COMMANDMENTS OF STORYTELLING

Inciting Incident: Paul Revere sparks the people of Lexington and Concord to prepare to fight the British. What do his actions look like in light of knowledge about Connectors, Mavens, and Salespeople?

Progressive Complications: They gather weapons and muster for the fight but are defeated by British Regulars in Lexington, with seven militiamen dying.

The Turning Point Progressive Complication: The British clash with militiamen at Concord.

Crisis Question: Will the preparation sparked by Revere's ride pay off?

Climax: Yes, The British are defeated at Concord.

Resolution: The British were defeated by a combination Maven and Connector who had Salespeople on his side.

NOTES

- This very short scene is another example of the importance of quickly bringing information already known to the reader into new, sharper relief before moving into new territory. This marks the end of one strand of inquiry and the transition to a whole new set of questions and stories in chapter 3.
- Because it marks the end of one strand of inquiry, Gladwell takes the time to craft an elegant, succinct summation: "[The American Revolution] began on a cold spring morning, with a word-of-mouth epidemic that spread from a little stable boy to all of New England, relying along the way on a small number of very special people: a few Salespeople and a man with the particular genius of both a Maven and a Connector."

CHAPTER 3 - THE STICKINESS FACTOR

SESAME STREET, BLUE'S CLUES, AND THE EDUCATION VIRUS

SCENE 23

641 words
"In the late 1960s, a ... how to make television sticky."
Summary: The creators of *Sesame Street* made television sticky to improve children's literacy.

INQUIRY EVENT

1. Literal Action: What is the author-protagonist literally doing in this scene?

Gladwell tells how Joan Ganz Cooney, Gerald Lesser, and Lloyd Morrisett of the Markle Foundation created Sesame Street *in the late 1960s.*

2. Essential Action: What is the author-protagonist trying to accomplish in this scene?

Gladwell wants to introduce Sesame Street *as an example of a positive social epidemic that demonstrates the Stickiness Factor.*

3. Life Value Change: What has changed along the Ignorance to Knowledge to Wisdom spectrum in the scene?

Sesame Street improved reading skills among children who watched, changing the external life value from Illiteracy to Literacy. Gladwell learns that Sesame Street *was founded as a sticky educational virus.*
Ignorance to Shoe-Leather Knowledge

4. Inquiry Event: What is the resulting Inquiry Event?

Can we understand the origins of Sesame Street *as an effort to make learning sticky?*

THE FIVE COMMANDMENTS OF STORYTELLING

Inciting Incident: In the late 1960s children from disadvantaged homes suffered from higher rates of illiteracy, spurring *Sesame Street's* creators to use television as a tool to combat poverty and illiteracy. How did they use television to improve literacy for children?

Progressive Complications: Good teaching is an interactive process, but television is a low-involvement medium, so the show's creators borrowed "sticky" techniques from television commercials, added animation to teach lessons, and used celebrities singing and dancing to increase children's involvement.

The Turning Point Progressive Complication: It worked! *Sesame Street* increased "the learning and reading skills of its viewers."

Crisis Question: Can Gladwell explain why this worked?

Climax: Creators made small but critical adjustments in how they presented ideas to toddlers and preschoolers, which overcame the "low involvement" quality of television and made the lessons memorable.

Resolution: "*Sesame Street* succeeded because it learned how to make television sticky."

NOTES

- As Gladwell opens a new line of inquiry into Stickiness, he returns to relatively upbeat, positive stories as illustrations.

SCENE 24

2,320 words

"The Law of the Few ... show it inspired, Blue's Clues*."*
Summary: Lester Wunderman's gold box campaign for Columbia
Records beat a more conventional ad campaign with greater exposure.
Howard Levanthal conducted experiments with high and low fear
messages.

INQUIRY EVENT

1. Literal Action: What is the author-protagonist literally doing in this scene?

*Gladwell tells two stories: 1) How Lester Wunderman handily beat the
McCann Erickson firm in a contest for a Columbia Records advertising
campaign, and 2) How Howard Levanthal conducted an experiment to see
whether high fear or low fear messages would convince more students to get
tetanus shots.*

2. Essential Action: What is the author-protagonist trying to accomplish in this scene?

Gladwell wants to demonstrate that Stickiness is as important to tipping a message as the messenger (Law of the Few), and to explain what makes a message sticky by presenting two examples of experiments with counterintuitive results.

3. Life Value Change: What has changed along the Ignorance to Knowledge to Wisdom spectrum in the scene?

Wunderman's method prevailed over those of the McCann Erickson firm, changing the external life value from Unproven to Proven. Gladwell learns that the nature of the message is as important as the messenger and that the elements that make messages sticky are surprisingly subtle and trivial.
Ignorance to Research Knowledge

4. Inquiry Event: What is the resulting Inquiry Event?

What makes a message memorable or sticky?

THE FIVE COMMANDMENTS OF STORYTELLING

Inciting Incident: The Law of the Few says that the nature of the messenger is important for the spread of a social epidemic, but Gladwell wonders about the nature of the message. If you can't rely on a big marketing budget, are there smaller, subtler ways to make a message stick?

Progressive Complications: Lester Wunderman proposed a contest between himself and the McCann Erickson firm to whom he was about to lose the Columbia Record Company's TV advertising contract. Wunderman used a cheesy gold box on the ads while McCann spent four times as much and reached more people.

The Turning Point Progressive Complication: Wunderman won the competition. Although conventional wisdom says that Stickiness should be a question of emphasis, small reach with a sticky message spreads while big reach with no Stickiness doesn't spread.

Crisis Question: Can we be more specific about what makes messages sticky?

Climax: In Howard Levanthal's tetanus shot high/low-fear experiment, he found a subtle yet significant change in presentation—unrelated to fear of the illness—caused students to get the shots. By adding a campus map showing where they could obtain the vaccination, an abstract lesson became practical advice about how the lesson could be *applied*. What makes a message sticky is often small and trivial.

Resolution: The information age makes Stickiness more vital than ever, but "there may be simple ways to enhance Stickiness and systematically engineer Stickiness into the message."

NOTES

- Gladwell chooses his examples carefully. Because the results in these two cases are counter to what conventional wisdom would suggest, we are less likely to conclude that some other force was at work, and we begin to accept the fact that often our intuition does not match reality.

SCENE 25

3,163 words

"Sesame Street *is best known ... sticky. The lesson wasn't.*"

Summary: *Sesame Street* creators made the show effective by testing episodes for viewer engagement.

INQUIRY EVENT

1. Literal Action: What is the author-protagonist literally doing in this scene?

Gladwell explains how Sesame Street *creators fine-tuned the Stickiness of the show by using data.*

2. Essential Action: What is the author-protagonist trying to accomplish in this scene?

Gladwell wants to show how the creators of Sesame Street *designed the show to overcome TV's passive quality and successfully teach their viewers by making minor adjustments to the presentation of the message.*

3. Life Value Change: What has changed along the Ignorance to Knowledge to Wisdom spectrum in the scene?

The creators of Sesame Street *made the show sticky by eliminating what made the show confusing to kids, changing the external life value from Unengaged to Engaged. Gladwell discovers that children focus (and therefore learn) when they understand the material presented.*
Ignorance to Research and Shoe-Leather Knowledge

4. Inquiry Event: What is the resulting Inquiry Event?

How did Sesame Street *creators make their episodes sticky so their viewers could learn?*

THE FIVE COMMANDMENTS OF STORYTELLING

Inciting Incident: The creators of *Sesame Street* set out to engineer the show to be sticky, or *memorable* to their preschool viewers. How did they accomplish this?

Progressive Complications: TV is a passive medium, not requiring understanding for adults to keep watching. Two studies showed that 1) children stop watching when a show doesn't make sense to them, which can be fixed by editing the episode, and 2) kids playing with attractive toys while watching remember and understand as much as kids who watched without the distraction.

The Turning Point Progressive Complication: Kids focus when they understand and turn away when they don't.

Crisis Question: What did the creators learn as a result of this revelation?

Climax: *Sesame Street* creators used the "Palmer's Distracter" to find out if kids understood the lessons of an episode. With this data, the creators made adjustments. The format was changed so that Muppets interacted with adults on the Street. The pun-delivering Man from Alphabet character was ditched. They shortened scenes to no more than four minutes.

Resolution: *Sesame Street*'s format and presentation came from a painstaking process to make the show sticky to viewers so the creators could be sure the children were learning.

NOTES

- This is another example of the Tipping Point lesson that we must test our intuition because reality and our opinions about reality are often inconsistent. Developmental psychologists said kids wouldn't like the combination of real and fantasy elements. But tests revealed this was definitely not the case. Kids disengaged when adults appeared alone. So the show was changed to allow Muppets to interact with adults. Similarly, successful Big Idea writers test their ideas to gain "procedural" and "perspectival" knowledge of their subject.

SCENE 26

3,146 words
"This was the legacy of ... in other words, Blue's Clues.*"*
Summary: *Blue's Clues* creators made a show that was even more successful than *Sesame Street.*

INQUIRY EVENT

1. Literal Action: What is the author-protagonist literally doing in this scene?

Gladwell tells the story of how the creators of Blue's Clues *made a show that was stickier than* Sesame Street.

2. Essential Action: What is the author-protagonist trying to accomplish in this scene?

Gladwell wants to show the reader how to improve on a format that is already sticky through the example of Nickelodeon's Blue's Clues.

3. Life Value Change: What has changed along the Ignorance to Knowledge to Wisdom spectrum in the scene?

Blue's Clues *viewers performed significantly better than the* Sesame Street *audience on cognitive tests, changing the external life value from Good Performance to Better Performance. Gladwell discovers that learning is story driven and that narrative rules!*

Ignorance to Research Knowledge to Higher Knowledge

4. Inquiry Event: What is the resulting Inquiry Event?

Can we understand how to make a story stickier than Sesame Street *by focusing on the core audience and the fact that learning is story driven?*

THE FIVE COMMANDMENTS OF STORYTELLING

Inciting Incident: In the mid-1990s, television producers set out to create a show that was stickier than *Sesame Street*. How did they accomplish this?

Progressive Complications: When *Blue's Clues* creators started working on the show, new research allowed for a better understanding of the way children's minds work. They applied this knowledge that children had longer attention spans than previously thought and that visual storytelling was vital. As a result, each thirty-minute episode employed one actor, one storyline, a slower pace, and no wordplay.

The Turning Point Progressive Complication: *Blue's Clues* beat *Sesame Street* in the ratings by a large margin, and *Blue's Clue*s viewers performed significantly better than the *Sesame Street* audience members on cognitive tests.

Crisis Question: How did the creators of *Blue's Clues* make the show (and its educational content) stickier than *Sesame Street*?

Climax: The creators of *Blue's Clues* paid even more attention to structure and format, fixing problems in *Sesame Street* that limited Stickiness for preschoolers. First, they eliminated the clever elements that appealed to adults but were confusing to kids (principle of mutual exclusivity). Second, they simplified the format with one central narrative, one adult actor, and a slower pace, based on the understanding that the narrative form is central to how children make sense of their world and experience.

Resolution: To make a show stickier than *Sesame Street,* Gladwell learns, "make it perfectly literal" and use stories to teach kids the way they teach themselves.

NOTES

- Like the creators of *Blue's Clues*, successful Big Idea writers include new information and adjust their hypotheses accordingly to gain greater knowledge and wisdom.
- An interesting thing to note about the structure of the book: The Middle Build Climax of *The Tipping Point* is about how children learn, and the Ending Payoff Crisis is about children in crisis. (See the Story Grid Foolscap)

SCENE 27

2,688 words

"Every episode of Blue's Clues *... often all that it takes."*

Summary: The *Blue's Clues* creators made adjustments to *Sesame Street*'s successful format to improve engagement and make Nickelodeon's show even stickier.

INQUIRY EVENT

1. Literal Action: What is the author-protagonist literally doing in this scene?

Gladwell tells the story of how the creators of Blue's Clues *constructed their episodes by leveraging the lessons learned from* Sesame Street *to make a show that was even stickier.*

2. Essential Action: What is the author-protagonist trying to accomplish in this scene?

Gladwell wants to show how the smallest adjustments in presentation to a message that is already sticky can make it even more memorable.

3. Life Value Change: What has changed along the Ignorance to Knowledge to Wisdom spectrum in the scene?

When Blue's Clues *creators layered show elements in the right order, children could watch repeatedly and learn more so they were more successful on tests, changing the external life value from Success to Greater Success. Gladwell learns that clue order is critical to making the message stickier.*
Research and Shoe-Leather Knowledge to Higher Knowledge

4. Inquiry Event: What is the resulting Inquiry Event?

How is Blue's Clues, *a show that beat* Sesame Street *in the ratings and in learning results among viewers, constructed for maximum effectiveness?*

THE FIVE COMMANDMENTS OF STORYTELLING

Inciting Incident: *Blue's Clues* creators borrowed elements from *Sesame Street* when they decided how to structure the show. But how did they change it to make their show more successful?

Progressive Complications: From *Sesame Street*, the creators of *Blue's Clues* learned that greater engagement made the lessons stickier, so they adjusted the format to allow for even more engagement: asking for participation, close camera point of view, and the "preschooler's pause." They also learned that repetition aids comprehension, so they repeated each episode for five days.

The Turning Point Progressive Complication: The creators learned that clue order is vital in making lessons memorable for kids.

Crisis Question: What can we learn from the fact that clue order matters so much?

Climax: The right order of clues allowed children to repeat each episode, which allowed them to absorb more of the educational content.

Resolution: Micro adjustments in the presentation of information to preschoolers changed the Stickiness of the information, which meant children learned more.

NOTES

- *Blue's Clues* succeeds as a story of discovery only if the clues are presented in the proper order. This is the trick to Big Idea books too. If you don't put the clues in the right order, the reader won't understand. *Blue's Clues* is a Nonfiction Big Idea Story in literary form. Compare the structure of *Blue's Clues* to the structure of *The Tipping Point*. The show has to start out easy to give viewers confidence. Then it gets progressively harder and harder, challenging the preschoolers while also repeating the clues. Gladwell does the same thing. This draws preschoolers and readers into the narrative. In other words, *you must progressively complicate the story of discovery and repeat core ideas.*
- The creators changed the *Blue's Clues* "Penguin" episode order from "ice, waddle, black and white" to "black and white, waddle, ice," and that made all the difference to children's understanding. *A small change* is often all it takes to make the idea sticky. The change moves the viewer from broad and global to specific, just like Gladwell's discussion of New York City crime in scenes 2 and 29 through 34.
- Paying attention to the order of information sets up narrative drive, pulling the preschool viewers through the same story multiple times and cementing the information for them.
- It's not surprising that changing the format of a story helps

kids learn more material. Story is an ancient psychotechnology that helps us make sense of the world, categorize information, and derive lessons from it.

SCENE 28

374 words
"There is something profoundly ... to do is find it."
Summary: Messages often tip not based on the quality of the message but the way it's presented.

INQUIRY EVENT

1. Literal Action: What is the author-protagonist literally doing in this scene?

Gladwell sums up the key points in the chapter, recalling the primary examples and connecting Stickiness to the Law of the Few.

2. Essential Action: What is the author-protagonist trying to accomplish in this scene?

Gladwell wants to "tell them what you told them," but also changes the resolution on Stickiness, going from microscope to telescope, so we see the big picture and its connection to Tipping Points.

3. Life Value Change: What has changed along the Ignorance to Knowledge to Wisdom spectrum in the scene?

The messages presented in this chapter tipped when the messenger paid attention to the form of the message, changing the external life value from Not Yet Tipped to Tipped. Gladwell learns again that the form of the message, or its Stickiness, is as important as the messenger.

Higher Knowledge to Wisdom

4. Inquiry Event: What is the resulting Inquiry Event?

What role does the presentation of a message play in its Stickiness?

THE FIVE COMMANDMENTS OF STORYTELLING

Inciting Incident: Stickiness doesn't work the way we think it should. What specific lessons about Stickiness can we gather from the examples in this chapter?

Progressive Complications: Wunderman's success is contrary to established principles of advertising. Levanthal's experiment indicates that a map was more useful than the hard sell to get students to obtain tetanus shots. *Blue's Clues* eliminated the elements of *Sesame Street* that made it exciting. *All counterintuitive!*

The Turning Point Progressive Complication: The Stickiness of the messages in these examples has nothing to do with their substance. The messages tipped because the presentation was adjusted—in very small ways.

Crisis Question: How do these results help us understand why messages tip?

Climax: The difference between a message that tips and one that doesn't is *smaller* than we think and has more to do with its *presentation* than its content.

Resolution: "There is a simple way to package information that, under the right circumstances, can make it irresistible."

NOTES

- Stickiness is about the message itself, but the content of the message, in other words its substance, didn't change in these examples. This turns the idea of a meritocracy in the marketplace of ideas on its head.
- This discussion is connected to two of the lessons of *The Tipping Point* in the Ending Payoff (scene 51). If we want to start positive epidemics, we must focus on a few key areas, but we also must test our intuition and our presentations to find the best approach.

CHAPTER 4 - THE POWER OF CONTEXT (PART 1)

BERNIE GOETZ AND THE RISE AND FALL OF NEW YORK CITY CRIME

SCENE 29

653 words

"On December 22, 1984, the ... a raucous impromptu street party."

Summary: Bernhard Goetz shot four young black men on a New York City subway in 1984.

INQUIRY EVENT

1. Literal Action: What is the author-protagonist literally doing in this scene?

Gladwell tells the story of how Bernhard Goetz shoots four young black men on a New York City subway in 1984 and is acquitted of charges related to the event.

2. Essential Action: What is the author-protagonist trying to accomplish in this scene?

Gladwell wants to introduce one of the two primary examples he uses to demonstrate the Power of Context again and show what life was like in New York City before the drop in crime he discusses at the beginning of the book.

3. Life Value Change: What has changed along the Ignorance to Knowledge to Wisdom spectrum in the scene?

Goetz shoots four young men, paralyzing Darrel Cabey, changing the external life value from Life to Life-Threatening Injury, and Goetz is acquitted of all charges. Gladwell knows the basic facts of the case but is left wondering why this happened.

Status Quo Worldview to Ignorance

4. Inquiry Event: What is the resulting Inquiry Event?

Bernhard Goetz shot four young black men on a New York City subway and was acquitted of all charges. In what context did this happen?

THE FIVE COMMANDMENTS OF STORYTELLING

Inciting Incident: Goetz carries a gun as he takes the number two downtown express train. Will he feel provoked to use it?

Progressive Complications: Goetz takes a seat next to four young men who are "horsing around." Troy Canty speaks to him. Barry Allen asks Goetz for five dollars. James Ramseur gestures toward a "suspicious-looking bulge in his pocket." As Canty repeats his request for five dollars, he smiles, as if he's enjoying himself.

The Turning Point Progressive Complication: Goetz pulls out a gun and shoots all four men, firing an additional bullet that paralyzes Darrell Cabey.

Crisis Question: Will Goetz be convicted for the shooting?

Climax: No, Goetz is acquitted of all charges.

Resolution: People celebrate outside Goetz's apartment.

NOTES

- The risk of death enters the book on the ground, with a specific example of crime in New York City, rather than the abstract statistics from scene 2.
- Within the details of this scene, we find elements that Gladwell later relies on to show that the Power of Context explains the behavior of all concerned in this case.

SCENE 30

702 words
"The Goetz case has become ... called a hero for it."
Summary: Crime in New York City tipped for the better in the 1990s.

INQUIRY EVENT

1. Literal Action: What is the author-protagonist literally doing in this scene?

Gladwell describes the depth of the crime problem in New York City in 1984 with specific details and also how crime dropped precipitously after 1990 to make New York the safest big city in the country.

2. Essential Action: What is the author-protagonist trying to accomplish in this scene?

Gladwell wants to establish the precise Tipping Point for crime in New York City.

3. Life Value Change: What has changed along the Ignorance to Knowledge to Wisdom spectrum in the scene?

In the 1980s New York City was in the middle of a crime epidemic. Soon after 1990, murders dropped by two-thirds and felonies by one-half, changing the external life value from Death to Life and Dangerous to Safe. Gladwell gains a clearer picture of the before and after details of the Tipping Point for crime in New York City but not why the crime problem tipped for the better.

Ignorance to Research Knowledge

4. Inquiry Event: What is the resulting Inquiry Event?

The crime rate in New York tipped for the better in the 1990s. Why did that happen?

THE FIVE COMMANDMENTS OF STORYTELLING

Inciting Incident: In the 1980s, New York City experiences one of its worst crime epidemics. What made it tip for the better after 1990?

Progressive Complications: Crime was bad above and underground, with 2,000 murders and 600,000 serious felonies in the city, including 15,000 felonies committed on the subway. Platforms were littered with trash, cars covered in graffiti, and the trains moved slowly through much of the city because the tracks were in disrepair. The MTA lost as much as $150 million in revenue as a result of fare beating. William Bratton described the subway as "the transit version of Dante's *Inferno*."

The Turning Point Progressive Complication: After 1990, crime in New York dropped. Two-thirds fewer murders were committed, and serious felonies dropped by half. By the end of the 1990s, felonies on the subway fell by 75 percent.

Crisis Question: The implicit question is, why did crime drop so quickly, and why so precipitously in New York City?

Climax: Gladwell doesn't answer the question yet.

Resolution: New York becomes the safest big city in the country. Goetz, who had become an important symbol while crime rates soared, was ignored during the civil suit brought by Darrell Cabey. By then, "It was simply inconceivable that someone could pull a gun on someone else on the subway and be called a hero for it."

NOTES

- In the book's introduction (scene 2), Gladwell told us that the crime rate in New York City dropped, and in this scene, he returns to the story and question of that scene. Why did crime tip for the better after 1990? Gladwell focuses on the moment when it tipped with a specific illustration of the change. Before crime tipped Goetz is a symbol; after crime tips, he's "almost an anachronism."
- Notice how Gladwell starts with New York City generally and then moves his focus to the condition of the subway (general to specific).
- The lost fares, litter, and graffiti in the subway system in the 1980s might seem irrelevant to the violent crime rate. After all, what do these nonviolent, nuisance crimes have to do with murder? But Gladwell is setting up his argument to show how the Power of Context contributed to the drop in the crime rate in New York City.
- This scene ends in a mini cliffhanger, one of the conventions of a Big Idea book.

SCENE 31

615 words

"The idea of crime as ... than we might ordinarily suspect."

Summary: Crime as a social epidemic doesn't make sense to us at first, but a deeper understanding of the Power of Context makes this idea easier to accept.

INQUIRY EVENT

1. Literal Action: What is the author-protagonist literally doing in this scene?

Gladwell reviews the lessons and examples from the first two rules of Tipping Points and explains that the change in New York City seems counterintuitive but makes sense in light of the Power of Context.

2. Essential Action: What is the author-protagonist trying to accomplish in this scene?

Gladwell wants to introduce us to the idea that the Power of Context applies to violence as much as it does to other epidemics. This is a setup for the hard news to come. Humans are sensitive to changes in the environment, which can cause even violent behavior.

3. Life Value Change: What has changed along the Ignorance to Knowledge to Wisdom spectrum in the scene?

The dramatic drop in crime meant that tens of thousands of people stopped committing crimes, changing the external life value from Law Breakers to Law Followers. Though it seems counterintuitive at first, Gladwell learns that the rules of epidemics apply to violent crime.
Cognitive Dissonance to Higher Knowledge

4. Inquiry Event: What is the resulting Inquiry Event?

Do dramatic changes in violence follow the rules of less serious social epidemics already discussed?

THE FIVE COMMANDMENTS OF STORYTELLING

Inciting Incident: Crime doesn't seem to make sense in regard to the three rules of Tipping Points as an epidemic subject. Is there a connection between crime and the disease and social epidemics described in *The Tipping Point*?

Progressive Complications: Other social epidemics Gladwell explores are straightforward, involving distinct messages or products. Crime is a collection of complex behaviors that don't seem to be contagious. "Criminals do not, in other words, sound like the kind of people who could be swept up by the infectious winds of an epidemic."

The Turning Point Progressive Complication: But for crime to drop the way it did by the mid-1990s, tens of thousands of people had to change their behavior to stop committing crimes.

Crisis Question: How can we explain this change?

Climax: The Power of Context explains why New York City crime tipped for the better. "Epidemics are sensitive to the conditions and circumstances of the times and places in which they occur."

Resolution: Gladwell realizes that people are extremely sensitive to changes in their environment, and as he explained in scene 4, the types of changes that cause epidemics to tip do not conform to conventional beliefs.

NOTES

- Gladwell spends the first two scenes of this chapter establishing the facts of crime in New York City, looking at it on the ground with the story of Goetz and at a high level from a statistical point of view. He employs a third-person omniscient point of view to present these facts. As readers, we can't argue with what is a matter of record. In the first paragraph in this scene, Gladwell uses first person plural to remind us that we are on this intellectual voyage of discovery together.
- Before Gladwell shows us in detail the changes that occurred to cause crime to tip in New York City, he acknowledges that there isn't an obvious connection between *crime* and *epidemics* or *crime* and *context*. It's as if he wants us to know he is, or at least was, skeptical too. He's playing devil's advocate and thinking critically about his ideas. This stance is not, strictly speaking, part of his credentials, but it does further establish *ethos*, bolstering his legitimacy right before he presents a very scary idea. Tens of thousands of people choose to commit violent crime—or not—because of small changes in their environment.
- Just like the order of clues was vital in episodes of *Blue's Clues*, the order in which the rules of Tipping Points are revealed helps us to challenge our previous thinking about

rapid and drastic change. But Gladwell's rules don't only progress according to what's more difficult to understand. The stakes are increasing too—from fashion choices to murder. If Gladwell doesn't structure his arguments this way, the reader could easily dismiss them, stop reading, and never get to the important ironic twist of the Ending Payoff about positive epidemics.

- Every few chapters it's essential for the Big Idea book writer to "tell them what you told them." Just like the repetition in episodes of *Blue's Clues*. But each example should also connect to and support the next idea or concept, adding layers of complexity to make the Big Idea stickier.

SCENE 32

3,338 words

"During the 1990s violent crime ... fact so hard to believe?"

Summary: The Power of Context explains why New York City crime tipped for the better in the 1990s, and it explains why a chance encounter on the subway led to the shooting of four young men in 1984.

INQUIRY EVENT

1. Literal Action: What is the author-protagonist literally doing in this scene?

Gladwell tells the story of how New York officials applied the Broken Windows theory of crime by cleaning up graffiti and cracking down on fare-beating and other quality-of-life crimes.

2. Essential Action: What is the author-protagonist trying to accomplish in this scene?

Gladwell wants to build his case that the Power of Context explains why crime tipped in New York City in the 1990s.

3. Life Value Change: What has changed along the Ignorance to Knowledge to Wisdom spectrum in the scene?

City officials applied the Broken Windows theory, changing the external life value from Dangerous to Safe. Gladwell learns again that little changes (fixing broken windows) can make a big difference.
Ignorance to Research Knowledge to Higher Knowledge

4. Inquiry Event: What is the resulting Inquiry Event?

How did application of the Broken Windows theory, focusing on small changes, contribute to the big effect of lowering the violent crime rate in New York City?

THE FIVE COMMANDMENTS OF STORYTELLING

Inciting Incident: Violent crime dropped in the United States in the 1990s in part because of a decline in the crack cocaine trade, the recovery of the economy, and an aging population. But these reasons for the gradual decline in US crime don't explain why crime in New York City dropped dramatically and rapidly. What accounts for the change there?

Progressive Complications: Subway director David Gunn applied the Broken Windows theory by eliminating graffiti on subway cars. William Bratton, hired to lead the transit police, focused on fare-beating on the subway. Above ground, Bratton focused on quality-of-life crimes.

The Turning Point Progressive Complication: The Broken Windows theory and the Power of Context are based on the same idea—that small changes in the environment can tip or reverse epidemics.

Crisis Question: If that's true, can the Power of Context explain what happened between Goetz and the four young men in 1984?

Climax: Minor elements of the environment, such as graffiti and other unpunished nuisance crimes, conveyed to both Goetz and his victims that their more serious crimes would go unnoticed.

Resolution: The Power of Context says we don't have to solve the big problems of crime to change it for the better because behavior is a function of little things within the social context. As a result, Gladwell says, the actions of the four young men had little to do with their background, and Goetz's behavior on the subway had nothing to do with his psychology.

NOTES

- Gladwell ends scene 31 by saying "the kinds of contextual changes that are capable of tipping an epidemic are very different than we might suspect." In this scene, he shows us this is the case.
- Gladwell references three crime stories that move our thinking from general to specific: 1) crime drops in the US because of broad long-term trends (crack cocaine, the economy, aging of the population); 2) crime drops in New York City because of local efforts to stop graffiti and fare-beating on the subway and other quality-of-life crimes in the city; 3) four young men on the subway hassled Goetz, and he shot them because the graffiti and chaos communicated to each participant that the environment was one of lawlessness and they would not be held accountable.
- This is another example that shows us the world operates much differently than we think. The New York City crime example suggests that criminals are not people who act for fundamental, intrinsic reasons, living in their own world, ignoring the social norms of society. Criminals are alert to subtle cues in the environment and act on them. What

Gladwell doesn't say, but is hard to miss, is that the rest of us are no different from criminals in this way.

- Gladwell finishes the scene by wondering why it is so hard to believe that Goetz's behavior was the result of subtle cues in the environment rather than his psychology. Gladwell invites the reader to examine their own thoughts on the subject. If we reject the evidence and reasoning, why is that? He addresses this in the next scene.
- This scene offers good news and bad news related to what it takes to change behavior. The good news is we don't have to solve big problems to decrease incidents of crime. Tackling small problems related to the environment can have big effects. The bad news is that subtle changes in the environment can tip dangerous behavior too.

SCENE 33

3,665 words

"In chapter 2, when I ... of me as fun anymore."

Summary: The Stanford prison experiment in the 1970s separated citizen volunteers into prisoners and guards in an attempt to find out why prisons are such terrible places. The Hartshorne and May cheating experiment in the 1920s tested thousands of school-age children on a variety of tests and conditions to try to measure honesty. Fundamental Attribution Error says that we tend to rely on character traits to explain human behavior instead of the immediate context.

INQUIRY EVENT

1. Literal Action: What is the author-protagonist literally doing in this scene?

Gladwell introduces two experiments that show how the immediate environment changes people's behavior (Stanford prison experiment and 1920s cheating experiment) and explains how they reveal our bias for using character traits to explain behavior.

2. Essential Action: What is the author-protagonist trying to accomplish in this scene?

Gladwell wants to understand how much influence the immediate environment has on the way people behave.

3. Life Value Change: What has changed along the Ignorance to Knowledge to Wisdom spectrum in the scene?

The way volunteer guards in the prison experiment treated volunteer prisoners was cruel and sadistic, creating "an atmosphere of terror" and changing the external life value from Controlling to Abusive. From the cheating experiment, Gladwell learns that children cheated based on the circumstances, not because they were "cheaters." This leads to higher knowledge that certain times, places, and conditions cause people to behave in ways they otherwise wouldn't.

Cognitive Dissonance to Higher Knowledge

4. Inquiry Event: What is the resulting Inquiry Event?

Does context really determine behavior more than background or genes?

THE FIVE COMMANDMENTS OF STORYTELLING

Inciting Incident: It's hard for us to believe that the immediate environment caused the Goetz shooting. Why is it so hard for us to believe?

Progressive Complications: In the Stanford Prison study, healthy and stable people responded to a prison environment by becoming abusive (prison guards) and by losing touch with their identity (prisoners). A person's immediate situation can drastically change their behavior, no matter their background or genetic makeup.

In the cheating experiments of the 1920s, children cheated because of the circumstances under which they were tested; honesty isn't a fundamental or unified trait.

The Turning Point Progressive Complication: Contrary to what we believe, people are capable of anything under the right or wrong conditions.

Crisis Question: Is there a way to understand why we explain behavior by relying on traits rather than context?

Climax: The Fundamental Attribution Error explains this phenomenon. People prefer to explain human behavior with "dispositional" explanations about a person's nature instead of contextual explanations because the former makes the world easier to understand.

Resolution: "Character isn't what we think it is or what we want it to be." When people seem to operate according to character, it is more likely that they are skilled at controlling their environment.

NOTES

- There is an element of "tell them what you told them" in this scene. Gladwell reviews what we now know but was counterintuitive about the Law of the Few (referencing Peter Jennings and the charismatic people examples) by way of setting up a similar explanation for the Power of Context. It is counterintuitive that small changes in the immediate environment cause big changes in behavior.
- Shawn Coyne mentioned this quote from *Chinatown* in his work on *The Tipping Point*: "You see, Mr. Gittes, most people never have to face the fact that at the right time and the right place, they're capable of ANYTHING."

SCENE 34

1,538 words

"Some years ago two Princeton ... was in a rat hole."

Summary: In a 1973 experiment, seminary students at Princeton were primed with the biblical story of the Good Samaritan and told either that they were late or had plenty of time to get to another place on campus. On their path they encountered a person in obvious distress, and the thing those who chose not to stop had in common was the perception that they were late.

INQUIRY EVENT

1. Literal Action: What is the author-protagonist literally doing in this scene?

Gladwell introduces the results of an experiment to replicate the Good Samaritan story among seminary students at the Princeton Theological Seminary.

2. Essential Action: What is the author-protagonist trying to accomplish in this scene?

Gladwell wants to show how the Power of Context applies to social epidemics other than violent crime, and when a person is predisposed to the social epidemic.

3. Life Value Change: What has changed along the Ignorance to Knowledge to Wisdom spectrum in the scene?

The behavior of most of the seminary students in the Good Samaritan experiment was ruled by conditions of their immediate circumstances (were they late for their appointments or not), not their personal convictions or the lesson of the Good Samaritan, shifting the external life value from Compassionate to Indifferent. Gladwell learns that the Power of Context applies even when people are not predisposed to the behavior.
Ignorance to Research Knowledge to Higher Knowledge

4. Inquiry Event: What is the resulting Inquiry Event?

Can small changes in the environment override a person's predisposition outside the context of crime?

THE FIVE COMMANDMENTS OF STORYTELLING

Inciting Incident: Darley and Batson conducted an experiment based on the Good Samaritan story among seminarians at Princeton Theological Seminary. Will people predisposed to helping others stop to help a man in distress, given different circumstances?

Progressive Complications: Each student was asked to prepare a talk on a theme and move to a different building to present it. Before leaving, the students were asked why they chose to study theology, assigned the Good Samaritan story or another subject as the topic for their talk, and told either that they were late or that they had plenty of time. While en route, they encountered a man who appeared to be gravely ill.

Almost everyone asked to predict the behavior of the students said that most would stop if they said they entered the seminary to help people and were assigned the Good Samaritan as the topic of their talk.

The Turning Point Progressive Complication: The only variable that significantly changed the outcome was whether the student believed they were late or early. Moral convictions were less important to the seminary students than their circumstances.

Crisis Question: What does this add to our understanding of the Power of Context?

Climax: Our disposition does not determine our behavior. The Power of Context is just as powerful in tipping different kinds of social epidemics as the Law of the Few and Stickiness. And we can alter environmental Tipping Points with small adjustments.

Resolution: The New York subway experiment and Stanford prison experiment say that people behave better because of the environment or context where they live and work. Goetz responded the way he did because he believed he lived in a combat zone, and the conditions in his immediate environment supported that belief.

NOTES

- In this scene, in addition to discussing the Power of Context, Gladwell tells us what he already told us, something every nonfiction writer must do. Epidemics tip because of the influence of special people (Law of the Few) and changes in the content and presentation of the message (Stickiness). In Big Idea books, it's important to repeatedly carry forward the core concepts and ideas that support the Big Idea.

CHAPTER 5 - THE POWER OF CONTEXT (PART 2)

SCENE 35

590 words

"In 1996, a sometime actress ... groups play in social epidemics."

Summary: Rebecca Wells and her successful novel, *Divine Secrets of the Ya-Ya Sisterhood,* illustrate a key principle of Gladwell's theory, the Power of Context. Specifically, Wells's story illustrates the critical role of groups in social epidemics.

INQUIRY EVENT

1. Literal Action: What is the author-protagonist literally doing in this scene?

Gladwell recounts how Rebecca Wells's book, Divine Secrets of the Ya-Ya Sisterhood, *went from relatively unknown to a blockbuster bestseller within two years of its publication.*

2. Essential Action: What is the author-protagonist trying to accomplish in this scene?

Gladwell wants to link the Power of Context with the role of groups in social epidemics.

3. Life Value Change: What has changed along the Ignorance to Knowledge to Wisdom spectrum in the scene?

Divine Secrets of the Ya-Ya Sisterhood sold fifteen thousand copies in hardcover, but within two years, the paperback hit the bestseller list and went on to sell 2.5 million copies, changing the external life value from Obscure to Bestseller. Gladwell notes that the Law of the Few (Wells is a Salesperson) and Stickiness (the story works and is well written) both contributed to the book's success, but he is confused and doesn't fully understand until he realizes the factor that had the biggest impact was the way groups operate in social epidemics within the Power of Context.
Cognitive Dissonance to Higher Knowledge

4. Inquiry Event: What is the resulting Inquiry Event?

Why did Ya-Ya Sisterhood *go viral?*

THE FIVE COMMANDMENTS OF STORYTELLING

Inciting Incident: Rebecca Wells published her book in 1996. Why was its success not immediate?

Progressive Complications: The book sold a respectable, but unremarkable, fifteen thousand copies.

The Turning Point Progressive Complication: When it came out in paperback, the book sold out in a few months, sparking the editor to take out an ad in *The New Yorker*.

Crisis Question: Can Gladwell explain what made the book go viral?

Climax: Yes, Gladwell understands and labels the reason the Power of Context, emphasizing the critical role of groups in social epidemics.

Resolution: Gladwell can now complete his explanation of the principles of social epidemics.

NOTES

- This chapter dives into the question of environment as a driver of change in new ways and explores the social and environmental mechanisms that Gladwell sees as most important in spreading ideas and information.

SCENE 36

960 words

"In a way, this is ... the course of social epidemics."

Summary: Gladwell analyzes the spread of Methodism to illustrate how the "skillful use of group power" helped make it more "contagious."

INQUIRY EVENT

1. Literal Action: What is the author-protagonist literally doing in this scene?

Gladwell explains how John Wesley grew Methodism through the power of groups, just like Rebecca Wells expanded the popularity and reach of her novel.

2. Essential Action: What is the author-protagonist trying to accomplish in this scene?

Gladwell wants to lay the foundation for how the Rule of 150 works in spreading messages.

3. Life Value Change: What has changed along the Ignorance to Knowledge to Wisdom spectrum in the scene?

Wesley was a Connector, but he wasn't a charismatic Salesperson. Instead of connecting individuals, he connected groups of individuals, changing the external life value of Methodism from Fringe to Popular Religion. Gladwell learns how small groups can amplify messages.
Research Knowledge to Higher Knowledge

4. Inquiry Event: What is the resulting Inquiry Event?

How do new religious movements take hold and become popular?

THE FIVE COMMANDMENTS OF STORYTELLING

Inciting Incident: Peer pressure operates within many groups. How do popular religious movements get started?

Progressive Complications: Methodism is an example of a quickly growing religious movement. It became an "epidemic" in the 1780s, but its founder was not the most charismatic preacher or a great theologian.

The Turning Point Progressive Complication: Wesley created religious societies—groups and subgroups of his converts—and visited them frequently.

Crisis Question: What do Methodism and the *Ya-Ya Sisterhood* phenomenon have in common?

Climax: Both depended on group culture and therefore were stickier and tipped into word-of-mouth epidemics.

Resolution: "The lesson of *Ya-Ya* and John Wesley is that small, close-knit groups have the power to magnify the epidemic potential of a message or idea."

NOTES

- This little chapter illustrates the power of small groups to magnify ideas and reiterates the Rule of 150, demonstrating that you can do a lot in less than one thousand words.
- We see Gladwell here doing a complex task of weaving together aspects of tipping that he has already explained, showing how one rule can enhance another rule. Social phenomena that are already sticky become even stickier when discussed in groups that are connected. And environment, or context, is also important to helping Wesley as a Connector.

SCENE 37

1,843 words

"There is a concept in ... good time to branch out."

Summary: There are connections between how our brain works and our social norms, including the "rule of 6 or 7" related to our "channel capacity" and our capacity for close emotional relationships (a rule of 12) and finally to the Rule of 150, which is the maximum number of people we can have meaningful relationships with.

INQUIRY EVENT

1. Literal Action: What is the author-protagonist literally doing in this scene?

Gladwell analyzes several external stories, all in some way about our "channel capacity." The most important is the story of the evolution of human brains. It's summarized in the quote from S.L. Washburn, saying that humans evolved in small groups to feel strongly about only a few people, short distances, and brief time periods.

2. Essential Action: What is the author-protagonist trying to accomplish in this scene?

Gladwell wants to prove the power of small groups (Rule of 150) is part of our evolutionary biology to bolster the rest of his arguments.

3. Life Value Change: What has changed along the Ignorance to Knowledge to Wisdom spectrum in the scene?

Social groups of a certain size allow "genuine social relationships," but when group members exceed this number, other mechanisms are required to maintain order, changing the external life value from Connected to Disconnected. Gladwell learns that the human channel capacity is 150.
Status Quo Worldview to Research Knowledge

4. Inquiry Event: What is the resulting Inquiry Event?

What size social groups are most effective in maintaining human connections and disseminating information (and why)?

THE FIVE COMMANDMENTS OF STORYTELLING

Inciting Incident: Gladwell learns the neocortex of human and primate brains is huge by mammal standards. How is this biological fact related to questions about human connections and relationships?

Progressive Complications: Some scientists think the neocortex evolved for food gathering. But that's proven wrong.

The Turning Point Progressive Complication: Studies show that brain size correlates with group size; the neocortex evolved to handle more complex social relationships.

Crisis Question: What is the maximum number of individuals with whom we can have genuine social relationships?

Climax: 150.

Resolution: Gladwell provides other examples of the Rule of 150, preparing readers to understand how the contextual element of channel capacity has an impact on social epidemics.

NOTES

- This is one of the most masterful of Gladwell's chapters because in a small space, he cites multiple scientific studies to support the power of small groups and leads the reader to believe in evolutionary biology as a determinant of behavior —something he'll call back to in the analysis of smoking. He suggests that the Power of Context is integrated into our biology.

SCENE 38

3190 words

"We have seen, in this ... book but to each other."

Summary: Gore Associates successfully employs the Rule of 150 to avoid the instability of change in large corporations. Gore succeeds through "bonds of memory and peer pressure."

INQUIRY EVENT

1. Literal Action: What is the author-protagonist literally doing in this scene?

Gladwell examines Gore Associates in Delaware to learn how it works so well without hierarchies and formal mechanisms.

2. Essential Action: What is the author-protagonist trying to accomplish in this scene?

Gladwell wants to connect the mechanisms that make small groups work —peer pressure and memory—to his search for the mechanisms that will tip an epidemic. He is still most interested in external environments, or contexts, and their influence on people.

3. Life Value Change: What has changed along the Ignorance to Knowledge to Wisdom spectrum in the scene?

The Gore Associates' secret sauce is the Power of 150. The company leverages peer pressure and memory systems by capping factory populations at 150, changing the external life value from Unstable to Stable. Gladwell learns that messages spread more efficiently among smaller connected groups, like the Ya-Ya Sisterhood *book groups and Gore Associates' factories.*
    Research and Shoe-Leather Knowledge to Higher Knowledge to Wisdom

4. Inquiry Event: What is the resulting Inquiry Event?

What mechanisms make the Rule of 150 work in a company like Gore Associates (or anywhere else for that matter)?

THE FIVE COMMANDMENTS OF STORYTELLING

Inciting Incident: Gladwell visits Gore Associates in Delaware. How does Gore avoid the change and disruption most large companies experience?

Progressive Complications: Bob Hen, Gladwell's guide, refuses to reveal his title and Gladwell is confused by the lack of hierarchy and why it works. He learns details of building size and how people work together.

The Turning Point Progressive Complication: Jim Buckley explains the peer pressure concept to Gladwell.

Crisis Question: Is there more than peer pressure at work, and exactly how does Gore really work?

Climax: Gladwell identifies, and Buckley confirms, the concept of global memory in the company. Gladwell backs this up with the study of global memory in families.

Resolution: Gladwell applies the Gore example more broadly to epidemics, seeing that new ideas and information move around more easily by using bonds of memory and peer pressure because of the Rule of 150. This transitions into his final truth of the chapter. "That is the paradox of the epidemic: that in order to create one contagious movement, you often have to create many small movements first."

NOTES

- Gladwell is able to introduce not only the idea of peer pressure that will be important in his later case studies but also the "small changes" idea as he further clarifies what exactly the Rule of 150 means. Each of the scenes in this chapter drills deeper into one central idea, discovering more critical evidence related to his central topic.
- Gladwell reminds us where we are in the larger argument at the beginning of the scene. We're looking at the Power of Context, and we've seen that small changes in the external environment affect our behavior. He recalls the earlier examples of graffiti's impact on crime and how the perception of lateness causes seminary students to ignore people in distress.

CHAPTER 6: CASE STUDY

RUMORS, SNEAKERS, AND THE POWER OF TRANSLATION

SCENE 39

875 words
"Airwalking is the name given ... the principles of epidemic transmission."
Summary: Airwalks, another brand of shoes that "tipped" in the 1990s, shows how epidemic transmission works.

INQUIRY EVENT

1. Literal Action: What is the author-protagonist literally doing in this scene?

Gladwell analyzes how the Airwalk company's shoes went viral in the mid-1990s, as a result of a targeted ad campaign to become "cool."

2. Essential Action: What is the author-protagonist trying to accomplish in this scene?

Gladwell wants to open an in-depth case study in order to demonstrate how the "principles of epidemic transmission" work on "less straightforward" problems.

3. Life Value Change: What has changed along the Ignorance to Knowledge to Wisdom spectrum in the scene?

The Airwalk brand tipped, with sales of $16 million in 1993 growing to $175 million in 1996, changing the external life value from Unknown to Popular. Gladwell learns that Airwalk tipped because of clever ad campaigns that leveraged Mavens, Connectors, Stickiness, and Context.
Status Quo Worldview to Research Knowledge

4. Inquiry Event: What is the resulting Inquiry Event?

How did Airwalk tip? The dynamic coordination of all the elements of social epidemics—specifically Mavens, Connectors, Stickiness, and Context— helps explain the phenomenon.

THE FIVE COMMANDMENTS OF STORYTELLING

Inciting Incident: Two entrepreneurs decided they wanted their shoe company to expand beyond hard-core skateboarders. How could they accomplish this?

Progressive Complications: The owners reorganized their business, expanded the focus to surfing, snowboarding, mountain biking, and bike racing, and embarked on a new ad campaign aimed at becoming cool.

The Turning Point Progressive Complication: The company hired Lambesis, a small innovative ad company, and sales grew from $16 million in 1993 to $175 million in 1996.

Crisis Question: Airwalk tipped as a result of the ad campaign, but what about the ad campaign made it tip?

Climax: The ads had all the hallmarks of a successful campaign, but more than their appearance caused the brand to tip. It happened because the advertising was founded on "principles of epidemic transmission" and relied on Mavens, Connectors, Context, and Stickiness.

Resolution: Airwalk is a good case study for how epidemic transmission of products and ideas works when more than one rule of Tipping Points operates.

NOTES

- This is just the introduction to the full explanation of Airwalk, so it teases the inquiry event without fully explaining.
- Gladwell revisits the concept of "cool" here as a setup to the next time he will use it with the problem of teen smoking.
- This is a turning point in the book and a great example of "perspectival" knowledge. Gladwell presents his big idea and the rules of Tipping Points in the Beginning Hook (propositional knowledge). In the majority of the Middle Build (scenes 10-38), he demonstrates and tests the rules with clear examples that highlight one primary rule of Tipping Points (procedural knowledge). In this scene, Gladwell turns to more complex examples of drastic and rapid change that illustrate different elements of the rules and how they work together (perspectival knowledge).

SCENE 40

2,115 words

"Perhaps the best way to ... rest of us can understand."

Summary: In multiple stories, ideas and products diffuse from small groups to large groups as Connectors, Mavens, and Salespeople work together to spread social epidemics.

INQUIRY EVENT

1. **Literal Action: What is the author-protagonist literally doing in this scene?**

Gladwell dissects several stories (about seed corn, technology, Hush Puppies, teen fashion trends, a Chinese teacher mistaken for a spy, and memory experiments with shapes) and introduces the concepts of diffusion, translators, and the leveling, sharpening, and assimilation of information.

2. **Essential Action: What is the author-protagonist trying to accomplish in this scene?**

Gladwell wants to understand why Lambesis's ad campaign was so effective by showing how social epidemics jump from the early adopters to ordinary people and how this relates to Connectors, Mavens, and Salespeople.

3. Life Value Change: What has changed along the Ignorance to Knowledge to Wisdom spectrum in the scene?

In each of the story examples, Gladwell demonstrates a product or social epidemic that tips to change the external life value from Unpopular to Popular within a particular context. Gladwell learns that Connectors, Mavens, and Salespeople translate messages and help social epidemics make the leap from a small group to a mass audience.

Research Knowledge to Higher Knowledge to Wisdom

4. Inquiry Event: What is the resulting Inquiry Event?

How do ideas and products become contagious enough to move from Innovators and Early Adopters to the Majority?

THE FIVE COMMANDMENTS OF STORYTELLING

Inciting Incident: Gladwell sees a gap he doesn't understand in many disparate stories: a gap between those who initiate or very quickly adopt something new and the rest of the larger group, which adopts the innovation later. What accounts for this gap?

Progressive Complications: In one example, hybrid corn spreads from innovators and early adopter farmers to other farmers because the larger group of farmers sees clearly how the seed performs. But other cases of social messages or epidemics are more complicated. Sometimes the innovators, early adopters, and the larger society have different goals and attitudes so that the message can't spread as easily.

The Turning Point Progressive Complication: Attitudes toward risk and ultimate goals differ between innovators/early adopters and the majority of people, creating a chasm that's difficult to cross.

Crisis Question: How does a message jump the chasm between innovators/early adopters and a mass audience?

Climax: Connectors, Mavens, and Salespeople serve as translators who "take ideas and information from a highly specialized world and translate them into a language the rest of us can understand."

Resolution: Gladwell makes the leap to generalizing from his case studies to all social epidemics. Connectors, Mavens, and Salespeople are the translators of social epidemics.

NOTES

- This chapter has an unusually large number of external stories, something Gladwell handles masterfully, but that may be difficult for many writers. He connects the introductory and concluding stories with one key idea— translation. A final short illustrative story about a Chinese teacher is literally about cultural translation.

SCENE 41

805 words

"There is a wonderful example ... that other addicts can understand."

Summary: Johns Hopkins runs a needle-exchange program in Baltimore in which super-exchangers (Connectors) efficiently and effectively act as intermediaries/translators between public health professionals and addicts.

INQUIRY EVENT

1. Literal Action: What is the author-protagonist literally doing in this scene?

Gladwell tells the story of how super-exchangers sold clean needles to addicts in Baltimore.

2. Essential Action: What is the author-protagonist trying to accomplish in this scene?

Gladwell wants to provide a new example of people who act as bridges or translators—this time between a small medical community and the majority of drug addicts, returning to his interest in the spread of disease and epidemics.

3. Life Value Change: What has changed along the Ignorance to Knowledge to Wisdom spectrum in the scene?

Epidemiologists working in Johns Hopkins University's needle exchange program discovered that some addicts were picking up used needles and selling new ones, changing the external life value of the addicts from Vulnerable to Safe. Gladwell learns that these super-exchangers are well connected and can bridge the gap between the medical professionals and drug users.
Status Quo Worldview to Shoe-Leather and Research Knowledge

4. Inquiry Event: What is the resulting Inquiry Event?

How do "super-exchangers" carry out their roles as Connectors to help drug addicts?

THE FIVE COMMANDMENTS OF STORYTELLING

Inciting Incident: A successful needle-exchange program begins in Baltimore. What accounts for the success?

Progressive Complications: Researchers want to analyze the program's success. They discover super-exchangers are collecting used needles and selling clean ones to addicts.

The Turning Point Progressive Complication: A researcher interviews super-exchangers to learn about why their role in the system works, discovering that incentives work well to spur translation of messages.

Crisis Question: Do we know what kind of people the super-exchangers are?

Climax: Yes. They are Connectors with knowledge and motives to bridge the medical and addict communities.

Resolution: Gladwell sees that the super-exchangers are ideal translators who provide a service the public health community cannot.

NOTES

- Note how powerful it is each time Gladwell returns to the real-life examples of the spread of disease because the link between social viral Tipping Points and medical viral Tipping Points stands out so clearly.

SCENE 42

2,041 words

"Lambesis's intention was to perform ... quickly in 1995 and 1996."

Summary: Dee Dee Gordon and the Lambesis advertising agency translated the hottest youth and alternative cultural trends for mass consumption by tweaking them—via leveling, sharpening, and assimilation—and put Airwalk on top of the athletic shoe market in the mid-1990s.

INQUIRY EVENT

1. Literal Action: What is the author-protagonist literally doing in this scene?

Gladwell explains how Dee Dee Gordon spots cool trends and suggests ways Airwalk can capitalize on them to become the cool shoe.

2. Essential Action: What is the author-protagonist trying to accomplish in this scene?

Gladwell wants to provide a clear example of the translation process via leveling, sharpening, and assimilation.

3. Life Value Change: What has changed along the Ignorance to Knowledge to Wisdom spectrum in the scene?

Airwalk rides "cool" translators to mass popularity, changing the external life value from Popular with a Few (cult following) to Popular with the Masses. Gladwell learns that Lambesis tipped the Airwalk brand by hiring Gordon to collect data on what innovators were doing and wearing, which the company translated for a mass audience.
Shoe-Leather Knowledge to Higher Knowledge

4. Inquiry Event: What is the resulting Inquiry Event?

How did Lambesis tweak cutting-edge ideas in order to translate them for mass consumption and sell a lot of shoes?

THE FIVE COMMANDMENTS OF STORYTELLING

Inciting Incident: Airwalk shoes clearly tipped after the Lambesis agency got involved. How did Lambesis and Dee Dee Gordon cause Airwalk shoes to tip?

Progressive Complications: Gordon observes and plucks examples of cool culture among trendsetters across the globe: men wearing makeup, James Bond, ironic country club culture, the Dalai Lama, kung fu movies, and many other phenomena.

The Turning Point Progressive Complication: Gordon suggests ways to associate Airwalk with trends by tweaking or lightening the ideas. Gladwell now understands that translation of ideas and products involves a process of leveling, sharpening, and assimilating.

Crisis Question: Does the leveling, sharpening, and assimilating process work to accomplish translation?

Climax: It usually works, but occasionally (the example of Tibetan monks cheating on a test) does not.

Resolution: The Airwalk brand became wildly popular because Lambesis successfully translated innovators' trendiness for a large audience.

NOTES

- Gladwell helps us see the connections between the insights he gained in the previous chapter and how the Airwalk brand spread in popularity. He unravels one of the stories in the chapter (the spread of a false rumor) in which "discordant details were leveled out, incidents were sharpened to fit the chosen theme, and the episode as a whole was assimilated to the preexisting structure of feeling and thought characteristic of the members of the group among whom the rumor spread." This is a reminder to writers that it's sometimes valuable to show your work by spelling out how you arrived at some conclusions.

SCENE 43

607 words
"The Airwalk epidemic did not ... would you ever buy another?"
Summary: The Airwalk brand falls because it stops being cool and innovative.

INQUIRY EVENT

1. Literal Action: What is the author-protagonist literally doing in this scene?

Gladwell shows how Airwalk loses the confidence of its core group of small shops and buyers and from there loses its aura of cool and its profits.

2. Essential Action: What is the author-protagonist trying to accomplish in this scene?

Gladwell wants to introduce the idea that simple word of mouth can lead to a downfall—in this case, the demise of profits for Airwalk.

3. Life Value Change: What has changed along the Ignorance to Knowledge to Wisdom spectrum in the scene?

The brand began losing sales, changing the obvious external life value from Popular to Unpopular. Gladwell learns that the Airwalk brand crashed because the company abandoned faith in its Mavens for the masses, and that the real external life value change was from Authentic to Inauthentic in the eyes of the most powerful customers.
Shoe-Leather and Research Knowledge to Wisdom

4. Inquiry Event: What is the resulting Inquiry Event?

What caused Airwalk's sudden demise? Why didn't the company last?

THE FIVE COMMANDMENTS OF STORYTELLING

Inciting Incident: Airwalk sales begin to drop in 1997. Why did this happen?

Progressive Complications: Airwalk failed to provide shoes to key locations during the back-to-school period in 1997, and distributors turned against them. The shoes were no longer innovative and took on a mainstream look.

The Turning Point Progressive Complication: Once the company gained success with a mass audience, it stopped giving specialty shops their own shoes, thus abandoning the core ethos of coolness.

Crisis Question: Can an innovative company built on trendsetting survive transformation into a company that serves the majority?

Climax: No. Once Airwalk stopped serving its core audience of Mavens, it failed.

Resolution: Airwalk's coolness and business strength died together.

NOTES

- Word of mouth made Airwalk and in the end also killed it. When the company abandoned innovation to court the Majority, the word spread that it was no longer an Innovator and no longer desirable for key consumers. Gladwell may be providing a cautionary tale for writers here. If we simply court the majority without providing innovative ideas in our books, we risk alienating our core readers.

CHAPTER 7: CASE STUDY

SUICIDE, SMOKING, AND THE SEARCH FOR THE UNSTICKY CIGARETTE

SCENE 44

1,037 words
"Not long ago, on the ... teenage smoking in the West."
Summary: A teenage boy named Sima dies by suicide. His death is part of a suicide epidemic that happened in Micronesia beginning in the 1960s.

INQUIRY EVENT

1. Literal Action: What is the author-protagonist literally doing in this scene?

Gladwell tells the story of a boy named Sima who died by suicide, an example representative of an epidemic of teen suicides in Micronesia. He analyzes the causes.

2. Essential Action: What is the author-protagonist trying to accomplish in this scene?

Gladwell wants to establish the teen suicide problem in Micronesia as a particular type of epidemic with specific characteristics and show that it is similar to another problem he's interested in—teenage smoking.

3. Life Value Change: What has changed along the Ignorance to Knowledge to Wisdom spectrum in the scene?

Sima and other young Micronesian teens died by suicide, and the epidemic tips to become widespread, changing the external life value from Life to Death. Gladwell learns how one boy's suicide became an epidemic, seeks help from an expert in understanding its causes, and in the end makes a connection to another epidemic.

Status Quo Worldview to Research and Shoe-Leather Knowledge to Higher Knowledge

4. Inquiry Event: What is the resulting Inquiry Event?

Why did one boy's suicide become an epidemic in Micronesia?

THE FIVE COMMANDMENTS OF STORYTELLING

Inciting Incident: A boy named Sima dies by suicide, and the details of the circumstances of his death mirror those of many young people between the 1960s and 1980s in Micronesia where a teenage suicide epidemic arises. What causes this epidemic to tip?

Progressive Complications: Teenage suicide in Micronesia becomes a "ritual of adolescence." The suicide victims have a lot in common. Young men in their late teens who don't suffer from depression and live with their parents take their own lives in a specific way and leave similar notes to explain their decision.

The Turning Point Progressive Complication: Gladwell consults anthropological research that says teenage suicides in Micronesia grew into a local ritual, engaged in by younger and younger boys, and the behavior developed "an experimental almost recreational element."

Crisis Question: Can we find some common characteristics of self-destructive behavior in teens by looking at teen suicide in Micronesia?

Climax: Yes. Suicide among teenagers in Micronesia becomes common and ritualized. It is, according to Gladwell, "a dangerous epidemic of self-destruction, engaged in by youth in the spirit of experimentation, imitation, and rebellion."

Resolution: Gladwell thinks the Micronesia suicide epidemic shares the hallmarks of the American teenage smoking epidemic—a contagious behavior of self-destruction, involving young people, as a form of self-expression and rebellion.

NOTES

- Notice how Gladwell starts this very difficult topic with the intimate, simple story of one young man and a gentler tone than he has used in other chapters about business or crime.
- By exploring the problem of teen suicide in Micronesia first, Gladwell helps the reader to see another problem, teenage smoking, from another perspective throughout the rest of the chapter. Offering a way for readers to compare a more familiar problem with a less familiar one can help lead them to the conclusions you want them to reach. This is another example of the pursuit of perspectival knowledge. As Gladwell shifts lenses to look at dangerous behavior in two different cultures, he gains a new perspective.

SCENE 45

534 words
"Teenage smoking is one of ... ought to fight the problem?"
Summary: The problem of teenage smoking is a confounding one, and current strategies have not been able to tip the epidemic for the better.

INQUIRY EVENT

1. Literal Action: What is the author-protagonist literally doing in this scene?

Gladwell introduces and analyzes the problem of teenage smoking through current research on the topic.

2. Essential Action: What is the author-protagonist trying to accomplish in this scene?

Gladwell wants to show how adults' basic assumptions about the teenage smoking problem make it harder to solve and to raise the question of whether the Micronesian suicide problem from the previous scene can offer insight into how to solve the problem.

3. Life Value Change: What has changed along the Ignorance to Knowledge to Wisdom spectrum in the scene?

Despite public health initiatives, smoking increased 73 percent from 1988 to the end of the 1990s (when Gladwell is writing the book), changing the external life value from Healthy to Unhealthy. Gladwell learns that the way adults see the problem of teenage smoking is wrong because they assume it's a rational behavior.

Status Quo Worldview to Cognitive Dissonance to Research Knowledge

4. Inquiry Event: What is the resulting Inquiry Event?

How might our conventional thinking about teen smoking undermine efforts to combat the habit?

THE FIVE COMMANDMENTS OF STORYTELLING

Inciting Incident: Teen smoking is a baffling problem no one knows how to solve. What if our assumptions about the problem are wrong?

Progressive Complications: Policy makers restrict advertising, increase prices, enact laws prohibiting the sale of tobacco to minors, and support public campaigns about the dangers of smoking.

The Turning Point Progressive Complication: These approaches have failed. Smokers don't smoke because they underestimate the risks.

Crisis Question: Does this mean adults should give up trying to stop teens from smoking?

Climax: No, adults should recognize that smoking isn't a rational behavior and in this way is similar to the Micronesian suicide epidemic.

Resolution: Current efforts haven't solved the teen smoking epidemic, but if adults could understand the true nature of the behavior and how it's similar to the Micronesian suicide epidemic, they could come up with better strategies.

NOTES

- Readers may see a subtle connection between this scene and an earlier one in the book. The teenage smoking problem is reminiscent of Howard Levanthal's fear experiments discussed in the context of Stickiness (scene 24). Knowing how bad tetanus is didn't change students' behavior, just as understanding the health effects of smoking hasn't made it less attractive to teens. In this case study, Gladwell draws on terminology and ideas introduced in the first half of the book.

SCENE 46

1,503 words

"The central observation of those ... endure years beyond his death."

Summary: A young man from an influential family on the island of Ebeye dies by suicide, and other young men on the island repeat his tragic behavior.

INQUIRY EVENT

1. Literal Action: What is the author-protagonist literally doing in this scene?

Gladwell presents university research evidence about how suicide can be contagious and tells the story of one young man from a wealthy family on Ebeye whose death tipped the epidemic on the island.

2. Essential Action: What is the author-protagonist trying to accomplish in this scene?

Gladwell wants to show how the Law of the Few operates in the Micronesian suicide epidemic.

3. Life Value Change: What has changed along the Ignorance to Knowledge to Wisdom spectrum in the scene?

One boy's suicide started an epidemic that tipped on the island where he lived, changing the life value from Individual Death to Epidemic. Gladwell learns that suicide can be contagious and operates according to the Law of the Few.

Status Quo Worldview to Research Knowledge to Higher Knowledge

4. Inquiry Event: What is the resulting Inquiry Event?

How does the contagion of suicide work?

THE FIVE COMMANDMENTS OF STORYTELLING

Inciting Incident: People who study suicide know that in some places and under certain circumstances one person's suicide can lead to others imitating the behavior. Can this explain what happened in Micronesia?

Progressive Complications: Sociologist David Phillips found a connection between news stories about suicide and suicide rates. Prominent suicide stories covered in the *Los Angeles Times* and *San Francisco Chronicle* were immediately followed by an increase in traffic fatalities. Phillips knew that one of the ways people die by suicide is by deliberately crashing their cars.

The Turning Point Progressive Complication: Suicides reported in the news operate as advertisements or permission in "a private language between members of a common subculture."

Crisis Question: Can this explain what's happening in the case of Micronesian teen suicides?

Climax: Yes. Suicide on the island of Ebeye wasn't contagious until a local celebrity, a young charismatic member of a wealthy family, killed himself. In the twelve years that followed, twenty-five more young people died under strikingly similar circumstances.

Resolution: The Law of the Few explains how the death of one boy, a Salesperson, caused suicide to tip on Ebeye.

NOTES

- In this scene, Gladwell makes his case in a straightforward way that is almost a mini Big Idea book in itself. The compact scene includes academic research (by experts for experts), a compelling story about a charismatic young man who comes to a tragic end (which reads like a novel), and a demonstration of how to understand suicide epidemics (Gladwell, the expert, teaches non-experts).

SCENE 47

1,601 words

"Does teen smoking follow this ... for driving the epidemic forward."

Summary: Several hundred people answer questions about their early experiences with smoking, and the results indicate that the Law of the Few operates in the teen smoking epidemic too.

INQUIRY EVENT

1. Literal Action: What is the author-protagonist literally doing in this scene?

Gladwell shares the results of his questionnaire about smoking and investigates to find a "smoking type."

2. Essential Action: What is the author-protagonist trying to accomplish in this scene?

Gladwell wants to learn more about why teenagers smoke in order to help stop this social epidemic.

3. Life Value Change: What has changed along the Ignorance to Knowledge to Wisdom spectrum in the scene?

Gladwell finds patterns in his unscientific questionnaire that are confirmed by academic studies identifying a smoking type, changing the external life value from Self-Determined to Manipulated. Gladwell concludes that smoking is perpetuated by charismatic Salespeople, a callback to the "Salesperson" teen who sparked a suicide epidemic in scene 46.

Ignorance to Shoe-Leather and Research Knowledge to Higher Knowledge

4. Inquiry Event: What is the resulting Inquiry Event?

Does teen smoking spread like other epidemics, through charismatic Salespeople?

THE FIVE COMMANDMENTS OF STORYTELLING

Inciting Incident: Given some of the similarities between teen smoking and teen suicides as reviewed in the preceding scenes, do the two social epidemics really follow the same logic?

Progressive Complications: Gladwell questions several hundred people about their early experiences with cigarette smoking. Patterns emerge that show smoking is associated with sophistication, and people consistently describe a permission-giver, or what Gladwell has labeled a Salesperson, associated with early memories of smoking.

The Turning Point Progressive Complication: Gladwell discovers that British psychologist Hans Eysenck found that hardcore smokers share qualities in common. They are extroverted, sexually precocious, rebellious, and defiant risk-takers. The more someone smokes, the more likely they will fit this profile.

Crisis Question: Can understanding smoking's Salespeople and the qualities of hardcore smokers explain why anti-smoking efforts fail?

Climax: Yes. Anti-smoking efforts fail because they try to prove that smoking isn't cool. But teens are attracted to smoking because the *hardcore smokers* they know are cool, not because the habit is.

Resolution: Smoking among teens happens because of the extraordinary influence of people who are cool, in other words, the Law of the Few.

NOTES

- In this chapter, Gladwell does something akin to his earlier trick of using his own friends as sources of research knowledge, but this time on a larger scale. He gains perspectival knowledge by conducting his own survey with a carefully developed questionnaire about smoking experiences. In a way, he's turning shoe-leather knowledge into research knowledge, and he's the researcher this time! This is something audacious and on brand for Gladwell but not often done by other Big Idea authors.

SCENE 48

1,482 words

"The teen smoking epidemic does ... turn all smokers into chippers?"

Summary: The problem with smoking is not that teens experiment with the habit, but that many teens become addicted. Contagiousness (cool Salespeople act as permission-givers) and Stickiness (smoking's addictive qualities) are two different and independent ways an epidemic can tip.

INQUIRY EVENT

1. Literal Action: What is the author-protagonist literally doing in this scene?

Gladwell presents the case for what makes teenage smoking dangerous. Its Stickiness means that some teens who experiment with the habit continue until they are addicted.

2. Essential Action: What is the author-protagonist trying to accomplish in this scene?

Gladwell wants to show how the Stickiness of the message and the influence of the messenger are different, which means the way to address each problem is different.

3. Life Value Change: What has changed along the Ignorance to Knowledge to Wisdom spectrum in the scene?

The danger involved with smoking is primarily a problem of Stickiness, which changes the external life value from Experimenting to Addicted. Gladwell learns that what makes smoking truly dangerous is its Stickiness.

Ignorance to Research Knowledge

4. Inquiry Event: What is the resulting Inquiry Event?

Should we address the teenage smoking epidemic by targeting Stickiness or the messengers of the contagion?

THE FIVE COMMANDMENTS OF STORYTELLING

Inciting Incident: Teen smoking is a public health problem not because they start, but because they continue. "The habit sticks." How does Stickiness work with the teen smoking epidemic?

Progressive Complications: Teens pick up the smoking habit because of contact with a messenger who is contagious, but they keep using tobacco for different reasons. Almost everyone dislikes the experience of smoking when they first try it, but some also experience pleasure from the experience, and those people go on to become addicted smokers.

The Turning Point Progressive Complication: Smoking's Stickiness depends a lot on the individual's initial reaction and "innate tolerances" to nicotine.

Crisis Question: Can understanding the reasons for Stickiness shed light on the failure of current strategies to prevent teens from smoking?

Climax: Yes. To tip the teen smoking epidemic for the better, we need to focus on what makes the habit sticky or what makes it contagious.

Resolution: Contagion, or the Law of the Few, alone, cannot explain teen smoking, and what makes cigarettes sticky is not what makes them contagious. So we must dig deeper to resolve the question.

NOTES

- When describing the syphilis epidemic in Baltimore (scene 5), Gladwell explained that the three things that cause the disease to tip were independent of one another: an increase in crack cocaine usage, decreasing availability of medical services in poor neighborhoods, and demolition of high-rise apartment buildings that were centers for crime and disease. Similarly in the teen smoking example, the Law of the Few (the cool people who smoke and inspire others to do so) and Stickiness (the addictive quality of cigarettes) operate independently of each other to tip the epidemic. Frequently, writers must decipher the interaction of multiple causes and effects.
- This scene sets up one of the lessons of Tipping Points (scene 51). Small, targeted efforts are the best way to stop negative epidemics and cause positive ones. Focusing on strategies that impact one of the three rules of Tipping Points (e.g., focus on Stickiness) is more effective than a general strategy aimed at the behavior (teenage smoking). In other words, identifying and tackling small problems is the way to affect an epidemic.

SCENE 49

1,335 words

"Let's deal with the issue ... teenagers want to do it."

Summary: Approaching the epidemic of teen smoking with the goal of making it less contagious is not an effective strategy.

INQUIRY EVENT

1. Literal Action: What is the author-protagonist literally doing in this scene?

Gladwell presents possible strategies to make cigarette smoking less contagious.

2. Essential Action: What is the author-protagonist trying to accomplish in this scene?

Gladwell wants to challenge conventional wisdom about why teens smoke.

3. Life Value Change: What has changed along the Ignorance to Knowledge to Wisdom spectrum in the scene?

Contrary to what parents believe, they don't have much influence over whether their teens smoke, changing the external life value from (parental) Power to Impotence. Gladwell learns that two possibilities for addressing the spread of smoking would likely fail because adults (and particularly parents) have little influence over their children or the contagious messengers.
Ignorance Masked as Knowledge to Research Knowledge

4. Inquiry Event: What is the resulting Inquiry Event?

How can we make smoking less contagious given parents' lack of influence?

THE FIVE COMMANDMENTS OF STORYTELLING

Inciting Incident: Is there a way to make teenage smoking less contagious by understanding more about the messengers?

Progressive Complications: Permission-giving messengers are less susceptible to adult influence than teen experimenters.

The Turning Point Progressive Complication: The studies of Judith Harris and David Rowe show that peers, not parents, have the greatest influence on children's lives and behavior.

Crisis Question: Can parents or other adults stop the spread of the smoking epidemic through strategies aimed at contagion?

Climax: No. Adults need to understand, "Teenage smoking is about being a teenager, about sharing in the emotional experience and expressive language and rituals of adolescence, which are as impenetrable and irrational to outsiders as the rituals of adolescent suicide in Micronesia."

Resolution: Talking to teens about the health risks of smoking is ineffective because the fact that adults don't approve of smoking makes the habit attractive to teens. Attacking the epidemic using parental messengers won't work, so Gladwell must look at other options.

NOTES

- As Gladwell points out on several occasions, there is often a disconnect between what we think is true and what actually is true. Conventional wisdom is often not wisdom at all. One of the lessons of *The Tipping Point* is how important it is for writers to question and test our theories and intuition.

SCENE 50

2,701 words
"If trying to thwart the ... sticky form of smoking possible."
Summary: Links between people who experience emotional problems
and heavy smokers suggest possible solutions to the problem of
smoking's Stickiness.

INQUIRY EVENT

**1. Literal Action: What is the author-protagonist literally doing in
this scene?**

*Gladwell presents options for solving the teenage smoking problem by
affecting its Stickiness.*

**2. Essential Action: What is the author-protagonist trying to
accomplish in this scene?**

*Gladwell wants us to understand that the way to solve the problem of
teenage smoking is to change its Stickiness so that experimenting with tobacco
doesn't have serious consequences.*

3. Life Value Change: What has changed along the Ignorance to Knowledge to Wisdom spectrum in the scene?

Gladwell learns that the way to combat teenage smoking is to focus on making sure teens don't go from chippers to hardcore smokers by 1) finding Stickiness Tipping Points and 2) adopting a reasonable approach to teenage experimentation, changing the external life value from Unhealthy to Healthy.
Ignorance to Research Knowledge to Higher Knowledge

4. Inquiry Event: What is the resulting Inquiry Event?

How do we make smoking less sticky?

THE FIVE COMMANDMENTS OF STORYTELLING

Inciting Incident: Trying to make teenage smoking less contagious is ineffective, but can Stickiness provide a solution for the teenage smoking epidemic?

Progressive Complications: The nicotine patch makes smoking less sticky for some but doesn't deliver the same hit as smoking. The connection between depression and smoking addiction reveals that the smoking habit may be vulnerable to a Stickiness Tipping Point. In the beginning, all teen smokers are chippers who smoke only occasionally, and most quit before becoming addicted.

The Turning Point Progressive Complication: There is a threshold or Tipping Point for nicotine addiction, and chippers are the people who never smoke enough to cross the threshold.

Crisis Question: Can these facts tell us anything about how to combat teen smoking?

Climax: Yes. Analysis suggests that the threshold for addiction is between four and six milligrams of nicotine, so changing the message or making it less sticky means keeping the nicotine level in cigarettes below the addiction threshold.

Resolution: The problem of teen smoking might be improved if we identify Stickiness Tipping Points and take a less hardline approach to teenage experimentation. Kids and teenagers experiment, and while clearly there is no safer form of suicide, there can be a safer form of smoking if we identify addiction Tipping Points and prevent "chippers" from becoming hardcore smokers.

NOTES

- In urging that we take a less hardline approach and identify addiction Tipping Points, Gladwell is battling the primary antagonist of the book again—human ignorance. In this case, if ignorance wins, people die.

CHAPTER 8: CONCLUSION

FOCUS, TEST, BELIEVE

SCENE 51

1,960 words
"Not long ago a nurse ... place—it can be tipped."
Summary: Georgia Sadler works to halt real-world epidemics in the black community in San Diego.

INQUIRY EVENT

1. Literal Action: What is the author-protagonist literally doing in this scene?

Gladwell investigates how Georgia Sadler created an effective grassroots movement to prevent diabetes and breast cancer by applying the lessons of Tipping Points.

2. Essential Action: What is the author-protagonist trying to accomplish in this scene?

Gladwell wants to show readers how to apply the lessons of Tipping Points.

3. Life Value Change: What has changed along the Ignorance to Knowledge to Wisdom spectrum in the scene?

Sadler's initial efforts weren't making the impact she'd hoped for, but applying the lessons of Tipping Points allowed her positive epidemic to tip, changing the external life value from Ineffective to Effective. Gladwell learns that it's not enough to know the rules of Tipping Points because tipping requires concentrated efforts in key areas.

Higher Knowledge to Wisdom

4. Inquiry Event: What is the resulting Inquiry Event?

How can we create positive Tipping Points?

THE FIVE COMMANDMENTS OF STORYTELLING

Inciting Incident: Georgia Sadler wanted to spread the word about how to prevent diabetes and breast cancer in the black community of San Diego, but her initial efforts—seminars in black churches—were unsuccessful. How could she be more effective?

Progressive Complications: Sadler applied the lessons of Tipping Points. She created a new context where women had time and energy and were receptive to hearing information (hair salons). She enlisted new messengers who were Connectors, Mavens, and Salespeople (hair stylists). And she developed a stickier way to present the information (training and information customized for the environment with "gossipy tidbits and conversational starters"). She tested her results to make sure her efforts worked.

The Turning Point Progressive Complication: Sadler's changes to the program worked.

Crisis Question: Can we glean lessons from Sadler's application of the rules of Tipping Points?

Climax: Yes. Sadler had a small budget and used it wisely. One factor that links several examples of positive Tipping Points is the use of small and focused actions. Sadler tested her results to make sure the program was working, proving that we have to reframe how we see the world because our intuitions about human communication are often wrong. (Final reference to the book's antagonist or villain.)

Resolution: The three lessons of *The Tipping Point* are 1) concentrate resources on a few key areas; 2) realize the world doesn't work according to intuition, so you must test the results; and 3) believe that change in the world is possible, that given "the slightest push—in just the right place—it can be tipped."

NOTES

- This is the optimistic how-to element of Gladwell's Big Idea book, and it answers the second question he asks at the end of the introduction (scene 4): "And what can we do to deliberately start and control positive epidemics of our own?"
- In this scene, Gladwell asks, "And how much easier is it to hang the hooks of knowledge on a story?" This is precisely what he does in *The Tipping Point*. The reader understands and remembers the rules and lessons because of the stories inextricably linked with them.

AFTERWORD

TIPPING POINT LESSONS FROM THE REAL WORLD

SCENE 52

5,338 words

"Not long after The Tipping *... is more important than ever."*

Summary: Gladwell steps back to consider what he's learned from talking to others and with a year's perspective after the release of *The Tipping Point*.

INQUIRY EVENT

1. Literal Action: What is the author-protagonist literally doing in this scene?

Gladwell returns to the topic of Tipping Points with new insights, taking his ideas about the spread of epidemics deeper and recognizing two important influences he had not fully explored before: isolation and immunity.

2. Essential Action: What is the author-protagonist trying to accomplish in this scene?

Gladwell wants to understand why the epidemic of school shootings is happening in the United States, expanding his theory of Tipping Points to account for other factors.

3. Life Value Change: What has changed along the Ignorance to Knowledge to Wisdom spectrum in the scene?

The school shootings epidemic changes the external life value from Alienation to Mass Murder. Gladwell learns we must beware of isolation and immunity and that our need for Connectors, Salespeople, and Mavens to guide us has never been greater.
Research and Shoe-Leather Knowledge to Wisdom

4. Inquiry Event: What is the resulting Inquiry Event?

How do our current states of 1) isolation from each other and 2) immunity to new information prevent positive epidemics from tipping and make it more likely that negative epidemics will tip?

THE FIVE COMMANDMENTS OF STORYTELLING

Inciting Incident: An epidemiologist helps Gladwell see that when a problem, like the AIDS epidemic, is both a biological virus and a social epidemic, we're better off focusing on the "beliefs and social structures and poverty and prejudices and personalities" that spread the virus. But how can that be accomplished?

Progressive Complications: The school shooting epidemic in the US shares some qualities with the Micronesian suicide epidemic: ritualized, dramatic, self-destructive behavior in teens that is extremely contagious. These negative epidemics are more likely to spread because teens have more ways to connect with their peers than with adults. The Internet and email make it easier to contact more people outside our immediate social group, which should foster connection, but these methods also lead people to tune out, making it more difficult to spread positive epidemics.

The Turning Point Progressive Complication: As people become more overwhelmed with information, they become more open to advice from people they respect, admire, and trust—in other words, Connectors, Salespeople, and particularly Mavens.

Crisis Question: If the answer to the problems of isolation and immunity is to find Connectors, Salespeople, and Mavens, is there a way to do that consistently?

Climax: Perhaps. Connectors are predisposed to connect, so that makes them easy to find; but Mavens are more difficult. Gladwell suggests Maven "traps," and describes several.

Resolution: As we face new epidemics, isolation, and immunity, applying the principles of *The Tipping Point* is more important than ever.

NOTES

- As mentioned in the Introduction to this volume, the most valuable lesson Malcolm Gladwell teaches writers is how to acknowledge and even celebrate our own imperfection. The wrong turns, moments of confusion, and periods of being lost in a thicket of information are to be expected—a necessary part of the process. That's not only okay, it's essential to cultivating wisdom, expanding and improving our worldviews, and elevating our understanding to new levels. That's what Gladwell's story—and your story—is all about.

ABOUT THE AUTHORS

LESLIE WATTS is a Story Grid Certified Editor, writer, and podcaster based in Austin, Texas. She's been writing for as long as she can remember—from her sixth-grade magazine about cats to writing practice while drafting opinions for an appellate court judge. As an editor, Leslie helps fiction and nonfiction clients write epic stories that matter. She believes writers become better storytellers through study and practice and that editors owe a duty of care to help writers with specific and supportive guidance. You can find her online at Writership.com.

SHELLEY SPERRY is a Story Grid Certified Editor, writer, and researcher based in Alexandria, Virginia. She used to work at National Geographic, so she thinks every book is better if it has a cool map, a dramatic landscape, or a lot of penguins. As a writer and researcher, Shelley works with nonprofit and business clients on environmental, labor, and education topics. As an editor, she specializes in nonfiction, helping authors tell true stories about the world. She agrees with Barbara Kingsolver, that "revision is where fine art begins." You can find her online at SperryEditorial.com.

NOTES

Introduction

1. "Malcolm Gladwell on Truth, Trump's Tweets, and Talking to Strangers," Channel 4 News, 44:18, https://youtu.be/on7Wjdl_qhM.
2. Shawn Coyne, "Hero, Victim, Villain," *The Story Grid* (blog), May 5, 2015, https://storygrid.com/hero-victim-villain/.
3. Malcolm Gladwell, *The Tipping Point: How Little Things Can Make a Big Difference* (New York: Little, Brown, 2000), 7.
4. Gladwell, 216-217
5. Shawn Coyne, "Storygridding Nonfiction," interview with Tim Grahl, *Story Grid Podcast*, podcast audio, January 27, 2016, https://storygrid.com/storygridding-nonfiction/.
6. Shawn Coyne, "Four Nonfiction Points of View," *The Story Grid* (blog), May 19, 2015, https://storygrid.com/four-nonfiction-points-of-view/.
7. Shawn Coyne, "Narrative Drive," *The Story Grid* (blog), January 5, 2016, https://storygrid.com/narrative-drive/.
8. Shawn Coyne, "What We Talk About When We Talk About Genre," *The Story Grid* (blog), November 13, 2014, https://storygrid.com/what-we-talk-about-when-we-talk-about-genre/.
9. Gladwell, 259.
10. Gladwell, 258-259.
11. Gladwell, 259.
12. Shawn Coyne, "The Five Commandments of Storytelling," *The Story Grid* (blog), January 8, 2015, https://storygrid.com/466/.
13. Shawn Coyne, "5 Commandments and Pheres," interview with Tim Grahl, *The Story Grid Podcast*, podcast audio, April 25, 2019, https://storygrid.com/5-commandments-and-pheres/.